DOABLE MIDSUMMER NIGHT'S DREAM

**William Shakespeare's
Comedy
In "Do Able" Form**

by

Brent Nautic Von Horn

DOABLE MIDSUMMER NIGHT'S DREAM

Copyright © 2020 Brent N. Von Horn

All rights reserved. Printed in the United States of America. No part of this book may be used or reproduced in any manner whatsoever without written permission except in the case of brief quotations embodied in critical articles or reviews.

This work may be performed before live audiences, provided a license to do so is obtained from Brent N. Von Horn prior to performance. See detailed information on how to obtain such license at the back of this book, or contact the author at:

Nautic Publishing

Brent N. Von Horn

https://www.nauticproductions.com

Cover design by Nautic Productions © 2020 Brent N. Von Horn

ISBN: 978-1-953479-00-6 (Paperback); 978-1-953479-01-3 (eBook)

First Edition, 2020

10 9 8 7 6 5 4 3 2 1

CONTENTS:

Introduction ii
Synopsis iv
Characters v
PROLOGUE 1
ACT 1 3
ACT 2 39
ACT 3 74
ACT 4 111
ACT 5 122
   Key Changes from Shakespeare's play 143
   Character Notes 148
   Set Design Notes 161
   Production License 163

Introduction

William Shakespeare is often revered as the Greatest Playwright ever. However, he lived 400 years ago and in modern times actors and audiences both have trouble understanding his plays. The English language was quite different back around 1600. Puns and rhymes don't necessarily work anymore. Shakespeare's references to current events (from the 1600's!) are meaningless to our ears. Shakespeare also had a penchant for waxing poetic, which many people love but just as many (or more?) find annoying and distracting to the story.

These "Do Able" versions of Shakespeare's plays are true versions of his works, still mostly using the Bard's words, but edited to be more easily comprehensible for modern audiences. Readers have provided feedback comments such as, "I never liked Shakespeare before, but this (*Doable Tempest*) was fantastic!" and "I hated having to read Romeo and Juliet in school. Thank you for taking out all the sucky stuff! *Doable Romeo & Juliet* is very readable, and now I see what a beautiful love story it is."

Shakespeare's plays were written in the years when bubonic plague epidemics ravaged London, and theatres were dirty places. The "players" who acted were all men, by law, as the stage was not considered suitable for women. Shakespeare wrote for the audiences of his time. He wrote for the low-browed, uneducated, illiterate masses, who wanted action, sex, bawdy insults, and scandalous subject matter. In the same plays, he also wrote for the high-brow elite, the educated and cultured top tier of his society, who appreciated poetry, love, and tales of honor.

The goals of this Do Able version remain the same, aiming at the right balance of both fun and art, as that balance has changed over the years since Shakespeare's time. For actors, plotlines are explained, character breakdowns are provided, and stage directions (not written down in Shakespeare's time) are provided. For audiences, the original text is adapted to make it more palatable to modern ears, while still retaining the magic and beauty of Shakespeare's writing. In practice this means the cutting of some minor characters, as well as many lines of dialogue where (measured by our short-attention-span culture) Shakespeare perhaps waxed a bit too poetic and strayed away from his plotlines and action. Some scenes are entirely rewritten. Some scenes are rearranged.

Be assured though, enough remains to be true to the original. If we've succeeded in writing this book, you will need nothing else in order to perform an outstanding production of William Shakespeare's *A Midsummer Night's Dream* with more clarity and effect than ever before.

Synopsis

Romantic triangles in which both the real and faerie worlds interact, resulting in a comedic mess.

Four young people from Athens enter the woods, where a mischievous fairy ("Puck") uses a love potion to mix up their emotions.

The fairy king uses the same love potion on his wife, to teach her a lesson – but instead learns a lesson himself.

When the love potion's effects are sorted out, everyone ends up happy. The couples wed, and at their wedding celebration watch a silly play (within the play), put on by the comic relief clowns.

Characters

Puck	aka Robin Goodfellow, a hobgoblin
Cobweb Mote Blossom Mustard	faeries in the service of Queen Titania
Oberon	King of the faeries
Titania	Queen of the faeries
Cheeks	their son
Hermia Lyle Helena Peter	four young lovers
Thaddeus	Duke, and Hermia's father
Breonna	Duchess to be, and Peter's mother
Philo	Duke's clerk
Nick Bottom Peter Quince Francis Flute Tom Stout Robin Starveling Snug	players
Extras	Faeries, Lords, and Attendants

A MIDSUMMER NIGHT'S DREAM

by William Shakespeare

PROLOGUE

Athens.

Enter Puck, addressing the audience.

PUCK
Gentles, calm yourselves and rustle not,
lest you lose the gist of our story and find your
wits in maddened confusion.
For as you entered this wondrous hall, I,
Puck, have upon you all a spell enchanted.
You might have sensed a change come over you,
like clanging chimes as the wind picks up, or the
feel of cool lapping waves on a baking beach.
Whatever your thoughts now, know that you are
wrong, that your eyes have long seen a world
that you thought was real, when not, and
endeavoring to open long-stuck eyelids now
may in fact just shutter your blinds further.
You've no doubt come to us with schooled
expectations of "thees" and "thous", "yons" and
"verilys" -- certain preconceptions of your
childhood tormentors, those arch educators with
hickory sticks!
But here shall you instead find nonsense
designed to mystify and please, as we tell our
story with practiced ease.
You -- most of you -- are mortals, with pitiful

senses, so I will start our story for you:
There once was a duke: Duke Thaddeus, the Duke of Athens (that's in Greece). Many years ago he left his wife for a night in the woods, where he was bewitched by the Faerie Queen, from which came their wild and untamed daughter, Helen. Duke Thaddeus has raised Helen as his ward alongside his own daughter, the fair and sweet Hermia.

At the same time lived a noble woman, Lady Breonna, far away in another land. She also spent a night in the woods, where the Fairy King, my good Lord Oberon, found her, and gave her her son, Peter.

When faerie kings and faerie queens dilly and dally with mortal affairs, the world's normalcy shatters asunder; up can be down, light can be shadow, and it all becomes so much fun for a hobgoblin like me!

But hark! Here come the Duke and his fiancée now.

(He withdraws.)

ACT 1

SCENE 1

Athens.

Enter Breonna and Thaddeus.

BREONNA
Oh! My lord, as we are not yet married, I must entreat you to slow your advances. What must your townspeople think, as you chase me here and there with such leering looks?

THADDEUS
They may think that I've outgrown my britches, for indeed there is a tightness of late.

BREONNA
Thad! Really! Proud stallion though you are, you must wait until our wedding night.

THADDEUS
Am I not Duke of Athens? Am I not he who makes the rules? I will have my way!

BREONNA
Not yet, big boy!
(They exit.)

SCENE 2

Outside Athens.

Cobweb, Mote, Blossom and Mustard enter and dance around Puck.

PUCK
How now, spirits? Wither wander you?

FAERIES
Over hill, over dale,
through brush, through briar,
over park, over pale,
through flood, through fire;
Around the wide and distant world
we do wander everywhere,
swifter than the moon's sphere.
We serve the Fairy Queen,
to spread dew upon her green.

PUCK
Be along, then. Do your dewery
while I find my own foolery.

(Blossom, Mote and Mustard dance, bestowing faerie magic and wonder everywhere.)

COBWEB
You are good at foolery, that I know.
You are that shrewd and knavish sprite called
Robin Goodfellow; the Puck who serves as King
Oberon's right hand, in all his wicked trickeries.

MOTE
Is this he, King Oberon's chief mischief maker? He
that frights the maids of the villagery?

BLOSSOM
The one that curdles milk and spoils roasts?

MOTE
Misleads night wanderers, as if a ghost?

MUSTARD
The one whom villagers call "sweet Puck"
when they hope to have good luck?

COBWEB
Long has it been since my Queen and her husband
separated, after fighting in jealousy over their
mortal loves, but I remember you.
I remember you well.

PUCK
Thou speakest aright.
I am that merry wanderer of the night.
Good Faerie King Oberon serve I.
No one is safe from Puck's sharp eye.
I jest to Oberon and make him smile,

Act 1 Scene 2

>while I a fat and bean-fed horse beguile.
>The wisest aunt, telling the saddest tale,
>no matter how old and frail,
>sometime for three-foot stool mistaketh me;
>then slip I from her bum, down topples she
>and "Oh my!" cries, while I steal the crust
>from her cooling cherry pies.
>
>### COBWEB
>There's to be a wedding here tomorrow. We are tasked with making this countryside and all within a lovely sight. That's why we've come, with our Queen Titania. She wants a mortal man, by name Duke Thaddeus, to be happy, for once he and my Queen were lovers and methinks the Queen does still carry a torch for him.
>
>### PUCK
>Ha ha! So that explains why King Oberon and I were drawn to this place!
>The world's natural magic has awoken strong, with sparkly dewy faerie beauty everywhere.
>We wondered what was up.
>
>### MOTE
>Our good Queen Titania has sent us out
>to flower the hills and water the glens.
>
>### BLOSSOM
>We tickle the frogs and excite the hens.

MUSTARD
We will with faerie dust brighten from above,
and make the whole world sing with love.

PUCK
Will you have time later for us to play our
own games of love under leaves dappled by sun
and moon?

BLOSSOM
Naughty boy!

(Blossom, Mote and Mustard exit.)

COBWEB
While our Lady quarrels with your king, we
faeries are to stay away from he and all his
creatures, so said my Lady. But, I might have
time to sneak away, and meet you, later.

(She exits.)

PUCK
This wedding-ready world, of a sudden,
looks indeed much brighter to my eyes!

(He exits.)

SCENE 3

Bottom's rug store.

Enter Philo, Quince, and Bottom.

QUINCE
Now sir, tell us true, what is the pay?

BOTTOM
And the audience? What chance we, simple town players, to become famous? Oh! Good courtly clerk! Tell us about the exposure.

QUINCE
And the pay.

PHILO
As you know, the wedding of my master Duke Thaddeus to his betrothed, the fair dame Breonna, is the event of the season. Be assured, only the finest nobles will attend. We must have the best players perform scenes of love and bravery and passion and mystery.

BOTTOM
Oh, I can do all that!

QUINCE
Good sir, you have not yet mentioned the pay?

PHILO
For players, none but the exposure.

QUINCE
None?

PHILO
But, hold your tears and whiny complaints! All shall be fed free food and wine, in the back. And the Duke has offered a purse of gold to the best group of players.

BOTTOM
That's me! Us! Us, I mean, of course.

QUINCE
What is in a purse?

PHILO
Sir … it is a very large purse.

QUINCE
Ah! Well, then.

BOTTOM
Good Peter Quince, we must begin immediately. Gather the other actors. Let us rehearse in the woods.

QUINCE
Good Clerk Philo, sir, do sign us up. We will have a most excellent piece ready for the Duke

Act 1 Scene 3

and his bride – a scene fit to celebrate their nuptials in the grandest style.

BOTTOM
A scene fit for kings and queens, though they of course be but duke and duchess.

PHILO
Very good. I will put you on after the sword swallower and his dancing pigs.

(He exits.)

QUINCE
Oh, no! We cannot tread the stage upon the leavings of pigs!

(Quince runs after Philo.

Enter Lyle.)

LYLE
Well met, father. How fared you in your acting meeting?

BOTTOM
Oh, Lyle. When will my son join me on the stage? I could force a part for you.

LYLE
Father, you know I have no talents that way. I'm afraid I inherited none of yours.

BOTTOM
Rug weaving is a fine profession, son, one which I am proud to leave to you. But a man should ever reach for something higher, should he not?

LYLE
Or should a man know his place in life?

BOTTOM
Never! What troubles you, son?

LYLE
Nothing, father. I am off to see friends.

(He exits.)

BOTTOM
(bowing)
Ahem … ahem. My lord, Duke Thaddeus, and the Duchess uh what's-her-name,
I, Bottom the weaver, am come before you – no, no, all wrong. Ahem … I, Bottom the weaver, forever now to be known as Bottom the star actor, Athens' own pride and joy, will perform for you. Too much? Ahem … Bottom the wondrous. Bottom the weaver-turned-player. Bottom the brightest light among dim bulbs. Bottom – Sir Bottom! Lord of the stage ….

(He exits.)

SCENE 4

Athens.

Enter Thaddeus and Breonna, with Philo.

PHILO
and forty-two. We have the cooks ready with the swallow pies you love so, sir, and the apple tarts.

THADDEUS
My god! Have you ever seen a woman so stunning? Breonna, sugar, your legs are the stems upon which perch the finest flower!

PHILO
You asked for entertainment, sir, so I've engaged a number of local acts. Should you like to hear of them? One blows bubbles larger than hens.

THADDEUS
What? Oh, no, thank you, kind Philo. But please, keep up the good work. My bride is to have only the most wonderful wedding celebration!

(Philo withdraws.)

BREONNA
Dear Duke, husband to be, let us speak again of

my suggested plan for your daughter, for you have not yet answered clear.

THADDEUS
I could think more clearly if you first helped me with this swelling problem I have.

BREONNA
Only one more day, dear heart. Now, focus. Your daughter Hermia shall one day rule the kingdom, as your true heir. Is not my son Peter the ideal husband for her? As I will be by your side, so my son beside your daughter.

THADDEUS
Peter is such a wild boy, and my daughter Hermia is sweet and mild tempered, and clean.

BREONNA
A perfect match!

THADDEUS
Uh, yes. But sweet tits … why don't we rest here, where no one can see us?

BREONNA
Let us finish our conversation. Hermia and Peter can be married upon the same day as we. Oh, what a party tomorrow shall be!

THADDEUS
But Hermia loves Lyle, the boy from town.

Act 1 Scene 4

BREONNA
Lyle! Why he's nothing but the son of Bottom the weaver. He's not at all royal.

THADDEUS
Neither is Peter royal.

BREONNA
Peter is my son, the son of your Duchess to be, which makes him practically royalty already.

THADDEUS
Lyle is sweet and loving to Hermia. I've long seen what a fine match they make, and it matters not what type of ass a son's father is.

BREONNA
Thad! I swear, I don't think you listen at all. Perhaps I need to rethink everything. You and I may not be right, this marriage misaligned, for what am I to do with my son?

THADDEUS
Oh! Don't talk like that! We are meant for each other, my candied love. Let us lay down together, here.

BREONNA
No, I must think. Thad! Stop it. I feel a headache coming on.

THADDEUS
Then lie down, you gorgeous creature, and let me massage you awhile.

BREONNA
Peter and I could go back to Troy. There is a ship departing tomorrow, and a good man I know there, with a daughter for my son, and I suspect a large greeting for me.

THADDEUS
What? Breonna, darling! Would you leave me unfinished, unsatisfied, my love dead on the vine? Would you take yourself away? And deprive my daughter Hermia of her happiness with your son? For I'm sure, she and Peter shall make a powerfully suited couple. They can rule together while we are off on travels, or just lying indisposed.

BREONNA
Really? Oh, what a sweet man you are!

THADDEUS
Come, lie your body beside mine.

BREONNA
Oh, but we have so much to do! We must prepare. Call them, do, right away.

THADDEUS
Surely, that can wait –

Act 1 Scene 4

BREONNA
(calling)
Peter! Peter! Hermia, dear!

(Hermia enters, dressed nicely.)

HERMIA
Good day, Mistress. Father.

THADDEUS
Ah, sweet Hermia! Sorry to interrupt. We can speak later. Feel free to return to whatever it is you were doing, elsewhere.

(From opposite enters Helen, muddy. She drags a large log with a beehive.)

HELEN
Father, I've found honey for your wedding feast!

(All on stage but Helen shy away from the bees.)

THADDEUS
(Aside.)
Bees! Now this has truly spoiled the mood.

BREONNA
Oh, we'll all be stung!

HERMIA
Helen! Must you always make a mess?

(Peter, muddy from head to foot, enters, following Helen.)

PETER
Hello, mother! Hello, good Duke, father to be. Can you believe this good fortune? I watched as Helen calmed the flying beasts and made off with their nectar, as if they were giving it as gift to her. Nigh a single sting has she!

BREONNA
Peter, here is Hermia, your love.

PETER
Oh, yes, of course, I forgot. Good day, fair Hermia.

HERMIA
(ducking the bees)
And to you, Peter. Father, may I go now?

THADDEUS
Eh? Might as well get this over. Come closer. We have much to discuss with you and Peter. Peter, come.

BREONNA
Oh, there's a bee!

Act 1 Scene 4

HELEN
Be happy, little sisters. Fly away and make more honey.

(The bees depart. From behind Hermia enters Lyle.)

LYLE
Psst! Hermia, are you all right?

HERMIA
Stay back, Lyle.

THADDEUS
(seeing Lyle)
You there, Lyle, come out of the shadows. I see you skulking about my daughter, Hermia, as usual. You have bewitched her with song and pleasant rhymes, coming and going 'round here with nary ever a greeting for me, and not once a "by your leave" – You two are no longer kids, are you? You've grown up together, but not once, Lyle, have you asked for my consent to court fair Hermia.

HERMIA
Your consent? Father, surely it is my choice, not yours.

BREONNA
By the ancient privilege of Athens, dear, a daughter belongs to her father.

THADDEUS
Yes. And he may dispose of her as he sees fit, according to our law and custom.

LYLE
(stepping forward grandly)
Ahem! Uh, Lord Duke, High Chancellor of all Athens, Ruler of –

THADDEUS
Oh, put a cork in it, Lyle. You are too late.

LYLE
Too late, sir?

(Breonna pushes Peter forward.)

PETER
Ahem! My good Lord Duke, High Chancellor of all Athens, Ruler of –

THADDEUS
A cork for you, too, Peter. Your hand in marriage to my daughter Hermia I've already pledged.

HERMIA / HELEN / LYLE
What?

PETER
Yes, what?

BREONNA
My son, it is all arranged. You and Hermia shall wed with us tomorrow! Go on, ask her.

PETER
(kneeling)
Hermia, will you marry me?

HERMIA
But I don't love this man!

PETER
Mother, I shall –

BREONNA
Rule Athens one day, alongside fair Hermia.

HERMIA
Father, I would you would but look through my eyes.

THADDEUS
Rather your eyes must with my judgment look. My law in Athens is absolute. I have spoken.

BREONNA
(aside to Peter)
Pounce now, son. No more dried potatoes for us. All we've ever wanted, all the riches of this kingdom, its diamonds and gold, all is within reach. Do not you let me down!

PETER
(to Hermia)
You are quite wealthy, sweet Hermia. No doubt, that is all Lyle sees in you.

HERMIA
And you, sir!

PETER
No, dear heart. I see a lovely young woman, coming into her prime, dressed as an angel should be. A flower, blooming in the first beams of dawn's early sunlight.

HELEN
Ah, Peter! Just as it was this morning, along the brook!

THADDEUS
Helen, be quiet. Adults are speaking. Thank you for the honey. Now, go take it to Cook.

HELEN
Yes, father.

(Helen drags the log. Peter helps her lift it.)

BREONNA
Peter, stay here awhile.

PETER
Helen needs help. I'll be back shortly.

(They exit, dragging the log.)

LYLE
Ahem. Sir. Lord and Duke –

THADDEUS
What is it, Lyle? Why are you still here?

LYLE
Your honor, Duke Thaddeus, sir. You must know, so I will tell you now. Sir, I have offered my heart to your daughter, Hermia, and she has accepted it. We are, ahem, betrothed.

THADDEUS
By God, you are not! Not without a father's blessing! What do you play at? Be gone. Get you hence before I become mad.

(Lyle exits.)

HERMIA
Father, it is so. We are engaged.

THADDEUS
Are you, really? Tell me, do you love this Lyle?
            (looking at Breonna)
If you love him, truly, then perhaps --

Act 1 Scene 4

BREONNA
The ship to Troy is yet at dock. Peter and I could ship as passengers this night, if we're not wanted here. Or with a word to the captain, I doubt not that Lyle should make a good sailor.

HERMIA
Lyle is a poet! A gentle man, even if not to gentles born. He is no sailor.

THADDEUS
Time and tide will make him so. Philo! Capture young Lyle and see he is loaded upon the ship, afore the mast as its newest sailor, in chains if need be.

HERMIA
No!

PHILO
Right away, sir.

(Philo exits.)

HERMIA
Father, how could you?

THADDEUS
Breonna and Peter shall remain here, with us, in their new home, where you and Peter shall make your happy family, and one day rule after me. By my rights as father, and as Duke, this is my

Act 1 Scene 4

decision, which I expect you to respect.

HERMIA

I do entreat your grace to pardon me.
I know not by what power I am made bold,
but I beseech your grace that I may know
the worst that may befall me in this case
if I refuse to wed Peter.

THADDEUS

Either to die the death or to abjure
forever the society of men.
Therefore, fair Hermia, question your desires,
know of your youth, examine well your blood,
whether (if you yield not to your father's choice)
you can endure the livery of a nun,
to live a barren sister all your life,
chanting faint hymns to the cold fruitless moon.

HERMIA

So will I grow, so live, so die, father,
ere I will yield my virgin patent up
unto Peter whose unwashed yoke
my soul consents not to give sovereignty.

THADDEUS

Take time to pause, and by the next new moon –

BREONNA

No, dear! Our wedding approaches with
tomorrow's sun!

THADDEUS
Oh, right. Hermia, darling. Take some hours to think it over. I must know your answer tonight. Come, Breonna. Let us walk under the trees, where I know of a lovely place one may in seclusion stretch out fully and nap.

BREONNA
I'm all yours, my love.

THADDEUS
Hurry!

(Thaddeus and Breonna exit.)

HERMIA
One night to think. One night to think about all the remaining nights of my life, be they happy and love-filled, or barren and cloistered.
This palace, my home of childhood joy, my courtly dresses. I've always thought that I would lead my people, after father. Athens is my home; these are my people. Can I flout its law?
Oh, Lyle! My heart cries out, but should not my eyes and mind decide my future?
A nun's life in cloister is not for me.
Oh, but this Peter! He doesn't even bathe. I shudder to think of his gnarly hands upon me, the taste of his woodsy breath, the earthly force of his filthy –

(Lyle re-enters.)

Act 1 Scene 4

LYLE
Psst! Hermia, it's me.

HERMIA
Oh, Lyle! You must flee the town. My father's men look for you, to force you to take a sailor's life!

LYLE
What? But I've never even been on a boat.

HERMIA
They care not, sweet Lyle. Father only wishes to rid his kingdom of your face, so that I may more willingly marry Peter.

LYLE
Ay me! For aught that I could ever read,
could ever hear by tale or history,
the course of true love never did run smooth –

HERMIA
This course will end in your blood,
if you do not make haste.
I can't bear the thought of the world losing you,
even if I must lose you and never see again.
You must run, now, to be free.

LYLE
Run with me!

HERMIA
I, run? Leave my home, my people?

LYLE
Ay me, but the weaver's son. I don't know what
I was thinking. I'm sorry, Hermia. Sometimes I
get caught up in my father's daydreams, but I do
well know my place.

HERMIA
No, Lyle! No! I meant no offense, my love. To
me, you are a prince of the royalest blood, better
than any such I've met. I meant only, however
should we live?

LYLE
Hear me, Hermia:
I have a widow aunt, a dowager
of great revenue, and she has no child.
From Athens is her house remote thirty leagues,
and she respects me as her only son.
There, gentle Hermia, may I marry you;
and to that place the sharp Athenian law
cannot pursue us. If you love me, then
in the woods a league without the town
meet me, where I shall wait in the moon's
shadows tonight for you.

HERMIA
My good Lyle, I swear by Cupid's strongest bow,
by his best arrow that truly goes,
by the simplicity of Venus' doves,

by all the world's forlorn loves,
by all the vows that ever men have broke
(Twice more than ever women spoke),
in that same place you have appointed me,
tonight in the moon with you I will be.

(Re-enter Helen.)

LYLE
Keep promise, love.

(He exits.)

HERMIA
Godspeed, fair Helen.

HELEN
Call you me "fair"? That "fair" again unsay.
Peter loves your fair. Your beauty, your easy
grace, your constant perfection. It's not at all fair.

HERMIA
Little sister, you can have Peter. I want him not.

HELEN
And yet, he's yours!

HERMIA
No, I leave him for you. Tonight, Lyle and I will
meet in the woods and flee this place, to be
happy together, far from here.

Act 1 Scene 4

HELEN
Hermia! Would you defy father?

HERMIA
I cannot be a nun, Helen.

HELEN
There must be other choices than that. Marry Peter, and all would be yours.

HERMIA
You take Peter, and the town.

HELEN
Sister, you know I am but a ward. I can't inherit father's title. That falls to you.

HERMIA
And yet, I relinquish it to you.

HELEN
My whole life, I've always been the ward, not the true daughter. The townspeople love you, not me. They call me a wild, untamed spirit, just because I love the outdoors. How fair is that? I wish I knew my mother. I wish father would speak of her.

HERMIA
I don't recall my own, she died so young.

Act 1 Scene 4

HELEN
And yet, your mother was of Athens, a rightful Athenian which makes you true born, and me the errant visitor.

HERMIA
Helen, you are too hard on yourself –

HELEN
No, you don't get it! Everyone stares at me.

HERMIA
Perhaps if you washed your hair, put on a dress –

HELEN
It's so easy for you!

HERMIA
Oh, that it were! Tonight I must flee what you say is this easy life.

HELEN
You could stay. Marry Peter.

HERMIA
I cannot. My love is Lyle.

HELEN
Will I ever see you again, sister?

HERMIA
I fear not, sister.

(They hug.)

HERMIA
I must go, at once. You are now the Duke's only
daughter. Remember me well, as I you.

(Hermia exits.)

HELEN
How happy some o'er other some can be!
Through Athens I am shunned, and she blessed,
yet it is she that flees and leaves all to me.
All but that I want, the love of the majestic Peter.
Love looks not with the eyes but with the mind;
and therefore is wingèd Cupid painted blind.
There is in Peter some inner voice that calls to me,
as if we belong together, whether he knows or not.
I can tell by his muddy exterior his joy of the land.
Peter is not born for courtly politics and duty.
He and I are free-spirited, born to run, to play.
I will go tell him of fair Hermia's flight.
Then to the wood will he this night
pursue her. And for this intelligence will he love
me, even if at first it is Hermia's eyes he seeks.

(She exits.)

SCENE 5

Athens.

Enter Quince, Snug, Bottom, Flute, Stout, and Starveling.

QUINCE
Is all our company here? I have with me your scrolls, by name and role, for the parts we are to play before the Duke and Duchess on their wedding day.

BOTTOM
First, good Peter Quince, say what the play treats on, then read the names of the actors, and so grow to a point.

QUINCE
Marry, our play is "The most lamentable comedy and most cruel death of Pyramus and Thisbe."

BOTTOM
A very good piece of work, I assure you, and a merry. Now, good Peter Quince, call forth your actors. Masters, spread yourselves.

QUINCE
Answer as I call you. Nick Bottom, the weaver.

BOTTOM
Ready! Name what part I am for, and proceed.

QUINCE
(handing a scroll to Bottom)
You, Nick Bottom, are set down for Pyramus.

BOTTOM
What is Pyramus – a lover or a tyrant?

QUINCE
A lover that kills himself most gallant for love.

BOTTOM
That will ask some tears in the true performing of it. If I do it, let the audience look to their eyes. I will move storms. No watcher shall stay dry. Now name the rest of the players.

QUINCE
Francis Flute, the –

BOTTOM
A lover is, though, part tyrant, yes? I may play a rough lover, with scowls more than tears. Do continue.

QUINCE
Francis –

BOTTOM
(as Pyramus, reading)
"With bells and shells a-tingle
I tarry to test my thimble."
Oh, good alliteration. Some of this is well written. Do proceed, Peter Quince; the actors are waiting upon you.

QUINCE
Francis Flute, the bellows-mender.

FLUTE
Here, Peter Quince.

QUINCE
(handing a scroll to Flute)
Flute, you must take Thisbe on you.

FLUTE
What is Thisbe – a wand'ring knight?

QUINCE
It is the lady that Pyramus must love on.

FLUTE
Nay, faith, let me not play a woman. I have a beard coming.

QUINCE
Your face is smoother than all else, and of all your voice is highest.

Act 1 Scene 5

FLUTE
(speaking low)
No it isn't.

BOTTOM
I could put on a mask and play Thisbe, too. I'll speak in a monstrous little voice: "Ah, Pyramus, my lover dear! Thy Thisbe dear and lady dear!"

QUINCE
No, no, you must play Pyramus – and Flute, you Thisbe.

BOTTOM
Well, proceed.

QUINCE
Robin Starveling, the tailor.

STARVELING
Here, Peter Quince.

QUINCE
(handing him a scroll)
You, with your clean but homely face, Thisbe's mother. – Tom Stout, the tinker.

STOUT
Here, Peter Quince.

Act 1 Scene 5

QUINCE

(Handing a scroll to Stout, and keeping the next.)

You, Pyramus' father. – Myself, Thisbe's father. – Snug the joiner, you the lion's part.

SNUG

A – a - a lion? Have you the - the lion's part written? Pray you, if it be, give it me, for I am sl-sl-slow of study.

QUINCE

You may do it extempore, for it is nothing but roaring.

BOTTOM

Let me play the lion, too! I will roar – "ROAR!" – I will roar such that make the Duke say, "Let him roar again." – "ROAR!"

QUINCE

And you shall do it too terribly; you would fright the Duchess and the ladies that they would shriek, and that were enough to hang us all. Snug will be tamer; a gentler lion.

SNUG

"arrrr"

BOTTOM

But I will aggravate my voice so that I will roar you as gently as any sucking dove. "MEOW!"

QUINCE
You may play no part but Pyramus!

BOTTOM
Master Peter Quince, I can be a lion, gentle and ferocious. I can be the lover, the tyrant, the damsel in distress, the rescuing knight. I'll thank you, sir, not to typecast me further. I am beginning to think that perhaps this venture is not worthy of my talents.

SNUG
Arrrr?

FLUTE
Without Bottom we have no hope of gold!

STARVELING
He took first in the hay wagon parade.

STOUT
His Hamlet last year was marvelous.

FLUTE
So, too, his Juliet.

(Bottom bows to them.)

QUINCE
Pyramus is a sweet-faced man, a proper

gentlemanlike man, the lead of our play, with his name billed first in the title. And he's in the entire play, so you cannot play a second part.

BOTTOM
Well, I will undertake it.

QUINCE
Masters, you have your parts. I entreat you, request you, and desire you to con them by tonight and meet me in the palace wood, a mile without town, by moonlight. There will we rehearse, for if we meet in the city, we shall be dogged with company and our devices known. I pray you fail me not.

BOTTOM
We will next meet in the woods, and there we may rehearse most obscenely and courageously, for who's to say what happens in the woods?

(They exit.)

ACT 2

SCENE 1

The Woods.

Enter King Oberon from above, scowling. Enter Puck from below.

PUCK
Oh, see how cross is my King Oberon!
That the woods are crisp with new-flung dew,
that each leaf sparkles in this moonlight so,
speaks clear to he and I: Queen Titania is near!
When last they met, typhoons and hurricanes
sprang forth, as they argued and squabbled over
his sleights and hers. For neither can the other stand,
husband and wife though they be.
Imagine that! Wedded bliss, yet constant strife?
As I am an honest Puck, honest to myself at least,
methinks it time to give him space,
to leave him fume in rage by self.

(Puck Exits.)

OBERON
Lady Titania, show yourself! Waste not

these moments of our wedded joy, for
I know you are near, as you too must know I
drift nearby.

>*(Oberon disappears in mist, and new mist forms below. Enter Titania and her Faeries, Cobweb, Blossom, Mote and Mustard.)*

FAERIES
Over hill, over dale,
through brush, through briar,
over park, over pale,
through flood, through fire;
Good Titania, Queen of the Faerie realm,
as you bid we did be-dew, be-sparkle, and be-joy
these woods from beech and oak, to farthest elm,
with heart-fresh love upon each girl and boy.

TITANIA
Well done, my girls. The good Duke Thaddeus'
wedding day shall befit the qualities of the man.
I fear now though the King, my husband,
Oberon, draws nigh.
I bid you quickly skip hence and go.
Leave me to deal with his rough bile.

>*(Faeries exit.)*

TITANIA
Well, Oberon, husband king,

though I have forsworn your bed and company,
I knew these events would us together bring.
Show yourself, you black-hearted troublemaker.

> *(Mist forms, out of which Oberon enters.)*

OBERON

Dear wife.

TITANIA

Husband.

OBERON

You look good, a sight for my eyes
which have not seen you for many years.

TITANIA

I do recall our last moments: you
throwing me about in your rage, the reach
of which sunk many ships and lasted an age.

OBERON

Oh, let's not rehash the past. I
hardly now remember what you did.

TITANIA

What I did?

OBERON

Come, be not like that. Your temper is second
only to your unfaithfulness.

Act 2 Scene 1

TITANIA

My temper? My unfaithfulness?
Oh husband, you've turned yourself into a mirror.
That you are here at this time is no odd fluke, no
coincidence. You've come to see your mortal fling,
the human woman Breonna, who just now is
betrothed to marry herself a duke. I trust you
come, too, to see her son Peter, the boy sprung
from your cheating loins.

OBERON

I did but exercise my manhood. One night. It
meant nothing. You, though. Be honest, wife.
Admit you are here because of your mortal fling,
your love for this human, this Duke Thaddeus.
You remember the time you cheated and your
resulting mortal daughter.

TITANIA

So, what of it? This was all begun by you. I only
saw the man because of your infraction, to make
you jealous. And I live with the consequences.
Long have I watched young Helena when she
comes to play in these woods. I've guided her,
and given her the gift of speaking with animals
and insects. You though, true to your ugly
selfish nature, you abandoned your son and not
once acknowledged responsibility.

OBERON

Responsibility? I am the Faerie king and do as I

please. No rape was there, nor force nor guile,
and what developed was then more her doing
than my own.

TITANIA
Foul man creature! Be gone! Go back to your
side of the world, the ice and snow, which best
befits that shrunken organ I once thought a
heart.

OBERON
You are but jealous.

TITANIA
Jealous? There is nothing to be jealous of.

OBERON
It is I that should be jealous, for you love the
man, and love the daughter.

TITANIA
I do. And though they mortals be, I still watch
over them.

OBERON
We need no longer continue this fight. The
power to end it lies in you.
Why should Titania cross her Oberon?
Do but apologize, to come back to my arms.

TITANIA
Let your arms stay empty some bit longer,

for you are still the same unchanged, unlearned,
unloving fool and away I go.

(Titania exits into mist.)

OBERON
That woman! Oh, how she fires me up.
What a woman, in truth! I could search for ever
and never find her like. How I love her so!
If only she put not her heart into her playthings.
Well, go thy way; but I know you'll not leave
these woods while young Helena plays about,
which means I shall find opportunity to torment
you for spurning me. Ah, I know just how.
Puck! My sneaky Puck, come hither; attend your
lord.

(Puck enters.)

PUCK
Here I am!

OBERON
Good and faithful Puck, come closer.
You remember where once we saw a mermaid
on a dolphin's back, uttering such dulcet breath
that the rude sea grew civil at her song?

PUCK
I remember the place.

Act 2 Scene 1

OBERON
That very time I saw (though you could not)
flying between the cold moon and the Earth,
Cupid all armed. A certain aim he took
and loosed his love-shaft smartly from his bow.
But as does sometimes happen, he missed the
maiden on first shot, and had to fire a second.
Yet marked I where the bolt of Cupid fell.
It fell upon a little western flower,
before, milk-white, now purple with love's wound.
Fetch me that flower.

PUCK
Flowers, lord?

OBERON
The juice of it on sleeping eyelids laid
will make a man or woman madly dote
upon the next live creature that it sees.
Fetch me these flowers, before the leviathan can
swim a league.

PUCK
I'll put a girdle round the Earth
in less time than sea monsters gallup so.

(Puck exits.)

OBERON
Having once this juice,
I'll watch Titania when she is asleep
and drop the liqueur of it in her eyes.

The next thing then she, waking, looks upon
(be it on lion, bear, wolf, or bull)
she shall pursue it with the soul of love.
And ere I take this charm from off her sight
(as I can reverse it with another herb)
I'll make her understand what it is to be led about
by the power of lust, to make her more forgiving
of me and less judgmental in her charms.
But who comes here? I'll be invisible
and stay to overhear.

(Oberon steps into mist and withdraws to the side. Enter Helen and Peter.)

PETER
I can love you not; therefore pursue me not.
Where is Lyle and the fair Hermia?
You told me they'd be here, yet all I find is
woods and woods, and more woods.

HELEN
You draw me, you hard-hearted adamant!
As sure as flowers draw bees.

PETER
Do I entice you? Do I speak you fair?
Or rather do I not in plainest truth
tell you I cannot love you?

HELEN
And even for that do I love you more.

PETER
I wish you'd return to town,
for I am sick when I do look on you.

HELEN
And I am sick when I look not on you.

PETER
You do impeach your modesty too much
to leave the city and commit yourself
into the hands of one you hardly know,
to trust the opportunity of night
and the ill counsel of a desert place
with the rich worth of your virginity.

HELEN
Your virtue is my privilege. I fear you not, Peter.

OBERON
(Aside.)
Peter? Can this be my son?

PETER
I'll run from you and leave you to the mercy
of wild and angry beasts.

HELEN
You would never let me come to harm, Peter.

PETER
Oh, Helen, if my heart were free. But you heard

my mother. I must for her find and woo the fair Hermia.

OBERON
(Aside.)
And this is Helena? Here we have both faerie-kissed children! Together, as they should be!

(Oberon extends the mist. Peter and Helen freeze all movement. Oberon draws near to Peter.)

OBERON
You are Peter, son of Breonna?

PETER
(woodenly)
I am.

OBERON
Know then that you are the son of the Faerie King, and thus faerie magic lives within your soul.

PETER
I have a father?

OBERON
Yet one would never know it by the cold and unkind way you spurn the love of this cute and friendly creature, the daughter of Queen Titania.

PETER
Who?

OBERON
Helena, whose loving energy is clear to see. You and she, being both faerie bred, are peas of a pod. How fitting that you find each other!

PETER
I must make my mother happy, so must I another woman woo. That way lies riches and gold, while with Helen is only mud.

OBERON
You have your priorities upside down, boy.

PETER
I had only my mother to teach me.

OBERON
Oh, ouch. You cut me deep. Return to your senses and I shall reflect on this.

(Oberon withdraws into the mist, freeing them.)

HELEN
What strange sudden mist.

PETER
What – is this real? It's as if I dreamed while

standing here.

HELEN
I dream of being yours.

PETER
Let me go, or if you follow me, do not believe
but I shall do you mischief in the wood.

(Peter exits.)

HELEN
Ay, in the palace, in the town, the woods,
you do me mischief. Fie, Peter!
We women cannot fight for love, as men do.
We should be wooed and were not made to woo.

OBERON
(whispering)
Do not lose heart, young maiden. Follow your
love.

HELEN
I know my path as if these woods were talking
to me. I'll follow, for in these woods all seems
magical, and where there's magic there's love.

(Helen exits.)

OBERON
Fare thee well, nymph. I have not been the father
I should have been, and it lies in me to make

amends.

(Enter Puck.)

PUCK
Good King Oberon, here have I your flowers.

OBERON
Well done. As Titania next beds down to rest,
with the juice of this I'll streak her eyes
and make her head swim full of embarrassing
fantasies.
She shall see what torment we men bear daily.
Take thou some of it, and seek through this grove.
A sweet Athenian lady is in love
with a disdainful youth. Anoint his eyes,
but do it when the next thing he espies
may be the lady. You will know the man
by the Athenian garments he has on.
Effect it with some care, that the two shall find
each other, for this pays a debt long overdue.

PUCK
Fear not, my lord. Your servant shall do.

(They exit.)

SCENE 2

Woods.

Enter Philo, carrying a large net. Enter Puck watching above.

PUCK
What fool is this? Could it be the Athenian my good King Oberon spoke of?

PHILO
Lyle! I know you are here. You can't hide for long!

(Philo swoops the net at a shadow, but captures nothing.)

PHILO
Come now, Lyle! The Duke has decreed that you are to be a sailor. Your ship awaits!

(He chases another shadow, then plops down to rest.)

PHILO
I followed Lyle this far, and stand ready to capture him and take him down to the ship, as my master bid me, but now these woods and tricky trees confuse and entrap me.

In truth, I think I'm lost.

PUCK
This can't be the one, surely. He seems too old,
and even more foolish than regular mortals be.

(Enter Hermia and Lyle.)

PHILO
Ah ha! Stand right there, young sailor man! My
lady, mistress Hermia, you should not be out here
in the woods!

HERMIA
It's Philo! Run, Lyle, or next you'll find yourself
chained in the hold of a ship!

LYLE
I cannot even swim!

(Hermia and Lyle exit.)

PHILO
Ahoy! Avast ye there, lubbers! It's time for you to
go to sea!

(He exits.)

PUCK
Who was that that he chases? A young man with a
girl? That must be he my good King Oberon told
me to find!

(He exits.)

SCENE 3

Woods.

Enter Thaddeus and Breonna.

THADDEUS
Here, my love. A perfect place to bed.

BREONNA
Oh, no. The branches appear too scratchy.

THADDEUS
We will hardly notice!

BREONNA
You would not, for you propose to lay upon me, right? It is I who must then lie upon the branches.

THADDEUS
Would you prefer the top?

BREONNA
Oh, Thad. I do not mean to be cantankerous. Is there not a blanket we could use?

THADDEUS
At home.
(She stares at him.)
But of course. Hold here. I shall return in but a moment.

(He exits.)

BREONNA
Well do I remember the last time a man had me in the woods, and what a man that was! Oh, 'tis a true shame Peter has never known his father. That was a man, let me tell you! A powerful figure, whose very essence was intoxicating. He swept me off my feet, and found ways to celebrate love I'd never even heard of. Aye, but in the morning he was gone, as men are prone to do. I have but his memory upon my fingers.

(Enter Oberon.)

OBERON
Breonna, I fear I have done you wrong.

BREONNA
Ah! Oberon, is it you? How can this be?

OBERON
I came when I heard of your pending nuptials, and then learned we have a son.

BREONNA
Well, if you'd come by earlier I would have told you.

OBERON
I abandoned both you and he.

Act 2 Scene 3

BREONNA
That's alright. You're back now.

OBERON
You are betrothed to marry another man.

BREONNA
No I'm not. Well, yes, but it's not yet done. Here, look. These branches make a nice bed.

OBERON
Breonna, I've come to apologize. My conscience is bothering me. These feelings of responsibility and regret are strange, being so new to me. Thinking with my upper head has never been my forte.

BREONNA
Lie down. You can apologize as we go.

OBERON
You're not listening. I'm trying to go down a different path, sweet and luscious Breonna.

BREONNA
This path is fine. I'll cushion the branches so not to make them too scratchy for you.

OBERON
You haven't changed at all, have you? Still so firm and sexy, and desirous.

BREONNA
Come closer and see for yourself.

OBERON
Oh, fie. What could a moment's diversion hurt?

BREONNA
(kissing him)
Yes. Take all the moments you need.

(Titania enters. Breonna freezes all movement.)

TITANIA
You pretend at conscience, but have learned nothing at all, you heartless monster!

OBERON
No, wait. You misunderstand. I was apologizing.

TITANIA
To her? You're supposed to apologize to me, you idiot!

OBERON
But she, you, I mean, no. This isn't what I meant to happen. Can you not forgive a man for simply following his nature?

TITANIA
Good riddance!

Act 2 Scene 3

(Titania exits.)

OBERON
No, come back!

BREONNA
(reviving)
I didn't go anywhere. Kiss me.

OBERON
(tearing free)
My lady, I must leave you.

(Oberon exits, following Titania.)

BREONNA
My Oberon, king of the forest, wait for me!

(Breonna exits. Thaddeus returns with a blanket.)

THADDEUS
Darling Breonna? I thought I heard voices. Where are you?

(Titania enters, speaking in Breonna's voice.)

TITANIA (BREONNA O.S.)
I'm right here, big boy.

Act 2 Scene 3

> THADDEUS

But, you –

> TITANIA (BREONNA O.S.)

It's me, your loving Breonna.

> THADDEUS

Oh. Yes. Yes, I see now. How silly of me. For a moment, I don't know what I was thinking.

> TITANIA (BREONNA O.S.)

Lay with me here, on these fine branches.

> THADDEUS

But I have a blanket.

> TITANIA (BREONNA O.S.)

Oh, aren't you kind, to think of me. Come, now. Rest your head. Lie here with me.
So long has it been, I'd almost forgot the sweet and tangy mortal smell of you.

(Enter Oberon. Thaddeus freezes all movement.)

> OBERON

Ah ha!

> TITANIA

Oh, "ah ha" yourself. You see how foolish you look?

Act 2 Scene 3

OBERON
Me foolish? It is you who foolish look!

TITANIA
I knew you watched! I did but play your actions in farce, to show your nature.

OBERON
This is the same mortal of before!

TITANIA
Cool your jealousy, husband. He's just a friend.

OBERON
Yeah? And then so perhaps is Breonna just my friend. In fact, I think I hear her near. I'll just go see my friend, and be "friendly" with her, shall I?

(He exits. Thaddeus revives. He kisses Titania.)

TITANIA
Oh, get off!

THADDEUS
Breonna, your voice has changed!

TITANIA (BREONNA O.S.)
Well, whatever. I'm not in the mood.

THADDEUS
How mercurial you are! You have me up, then

down, then up, then down, like a yo-yo.

TITANIA
That's your problem.

(Titania exits.)

THADDEUS
What game is this? I admit, I'm rather turned on by the strange voice trick. Breonna, I will catch you, my dear!

(He exits.)

SCENE 4

Woods.

Enter Puck and Cobweb.

COBWEB
Hello, again, Robin Goodfellow. I thought we might meet here.

PUCK
Cobweb, sweet faerie! Well met! And thank you for using my rightful name; I have grown well used to everyone calling me just "Puck." Are you finished working for your queen?

Act 2 Scene 4

COBWEB
For the nonce.

PUCK
I am on a mission now, to find an Athenian for whom the juice of these lovespell flowers is meant.

COBWEB
That sounds fun. There are two Athenians just over that way. But Robin, my Queen forbids us faeries to be near the King, or any of the King's men.

PUCK
Our duty first, as I must now hurry off.

COBWEB
Robin? Don't you miss me? Can you have forgotten what love we had those years ago?

PUCK
I do remember, Cobweb. But my King has bid me hurry.

COBWEB
Have you no more love?

PUCK
I am on a mission!

COBWEB
Go then, you Puck!

(She exits.)

PUCK
There it is. That name is often hurled at me so.

(He exits.)

SCENE 5

Woods.

Hermia and Lyle.

LYLE
Fair love, you faint with wand'ring in the wood.
And to speak truth, I have forgot our way.
We'll rest here, Hermia, if you're too tired,
and resume our trek in the morning sun.

HERMIA
Yes, be it so, Lyle. Find you a bed,
for I upon this bank will rest my head.

LYLE
One turf shall serve as pillow for us both.

HERMIA
Nay, Lyle. We are not yet wed and may not

yet flaunt conventions, even in the woods.
Lie further off. Do not lie so near.

LYLE

Oh, take the sense, sweet, of my innocence!
We are tired, and the night may further cool. Let
us share this spot and bring comfort to our bones.

HERMIA

Lyle, gentle friend, for love and courtesy,
lie further off in human modesty.
Such separation becomes a virtuous bachelor.
So be distant; and good night, my sweet friend.

LYLE

A friend's distance it is.
Here is my bed, then. Good night, dear friend.

HERMIA

I do love you so!

(They sleep. Puck enters.)

PUCK

Through the forest have I searched, but
as yet found no one in Athenian garb.
Ah! But here lies sleeping maid, and these clothes
indeed of Athens do speak loudly, yet was not my
master clear I am to find a man?
Why sleeps this woman all alone, in dark woods?
Oh, look! She has company, but though it is she
with better pillow, this churl sleeps far away.

He cares not enough for young maiden.
Churl, upon your eyes I throw
all the power this charm bestow.
>	*(He anoints Lyle's eyelids.)*
When you wake, your love will land upon the first
you see, and may it lead to warmer nights.

>	*(He exits. Enter Peter.)*

PETER
Do not haunt me so!

>	*(Enter Helen, running after Peter.)*

HELEN
Oh, will you leave me in the dark? Do not so.

PETER
Stay, on your peril. I alone will go.

>	*(Peter exits.)*

HELEN
Though I love these woods and can catch most
running deer, still this Peter is more fleet of foot;
I am out of breath in this fond chase.
Why does he run so? My face does not attract, on
its own, the way does the face of fair Hermia, with
her fine locks and blessèd eyes. How came her
eyes so bright? Not with salt tears. If so, my eyes
are oftener washed than hers.

Act 2 Scene 5

No, no, I am as ugly as a bear, if the reaction of
people around me be my judge.
But who is here? Lyle, on the ground!
Dead? I see no wound, no blood.
Oh Lyle! Wake up, if you but sleep.

LYLE
I wake, and will run through fire for thy sweet
sake.

HELEN
What?

LYLE
Your beauty radiates from above me, like sun rays
warming up the forest floor.

HELEN
Wake up, Lyle. You do still dream. This is not
Hermia's face you see. I am but Helen.

LYLE
Well do I see the true form above me.
You are your father's ward, yet so much truer
than his daughter in honest wholesome beauty
which lies far deeper than the skin's mere
reflection upon the eyes.

HELEN
No, Lyle, you mustn't talk so, though your speech
I admit does thrill as much as mystify my ears.
Your love is Hermia, and mine Peter.

LYLE
(jumping up)
Where is Peter? Oh, how fit a word
is that vile name to perish on my sword!

HELEN
Do not say so, Lyle, say not so.
What though he love your Hermia? That is but a
feint, to please his mother's goals and not his own
true meaning, deeper than his upbringing. Do not
label Peter as rival for your love. Peter will soon
drop his pursuit, and leave you content with your
fair Hermia.

LYLE
Content with Hermia? Never! I do repent
the tedious minutes with her I have spent.
Not Hermia, but Helen do I love.
Who will not change a raven for a dove?

HELEN
Wherefore do I deserve this scorn?
Is't not enough that Peter should run, but
now you must flout my insufficiency?
You do me wrong, in truth you do,
in such disdainful manner me to woo.
But fare you well. Perforce I must confess,
I thought you better than this, to play your games
at my expense.

(She exits.)

Act 2 Scene 5

LYLE

She saw not Hermia, sleeping there.
Hermia, my childhood crush, my playmate of younger years. Now my eyes have opened.
Things growing are not ripe until their season;
so I, being young, till now ripe not to reason
that my better match is Helen not Hermia.

(Hermia wakes.)

HERMIA

Huh? Did someone call?

LYLE

A snake you appear to me now!
A snake most heinous, wrapped around me, from which I flee!

(He exits.)

HERMIA

(she jumps up, screaming)

A snake, a snake! Lyle, help me!
Oh, 'tis but a nightmare; there is no serpent here.
But nor is anyone here; where is Lyle?
What, out of hearing? Gone? No sound, no word?
Lyle! Speak, if you are near! Speak, love, speak to me! I swoon almost with fear, to think you'd leave me here.
No? Then I well perceive you are not nigh.
Either death or you I'll find immediately.

(She exits.)

SCENE 6

Woods.

Enter Titania and Faeries.

TITANIA
Well done, my Faeries all, well done! The woods are bright with love and faerie dust, and on the morrow shall we dance all day to help the Duke celebrate his wedding feast –

THADDEUS (O.S.)
My darling, am I getting warm? Sing out if you hear me call!

COBWEB
My Lady, it is a mortal!

TITANIA
Oh, for toadstool's sake.

(Thaddeus enters and sees Titania.)

THADDEUS
Oh! I beg your pardon; you are not Breonna. But, hold! My god! Are you not that same wondrous and magical creature who loved me so long ago, and left me with the care of my little Helen?

TITANIA
Helena. I told you, Helena. Say not Helen; it sounds so human.

THADDEUS
Have you been out here all this time? To think, I had but to wander in the woods and here you'd be! This is wonderful! I was about to marry someone else, but now --

TITANIA
Oh, do shush and find some sleep.

> *(She motions, and Thaddeus drops sound asleep. The Faeries drag him to the side.)*

MUSTARD
Why must mortals eat so much? They will someday sink into the earth.

MOTE
Silly. Of course they will, as they are mortal.

BLOSSOM
And fat, she meant. Fat and heavy.

COBWEB
He can sleep over here, far from our Queen.

TITANTIA
Come now, 'tis late and my eyes heavy.

Forget that man, for he no harm can do.
Sing me now to sleep. Then fly you off to your
offices and let me rest.

> *(She lies down. Faeries begin dancing around her, in ever widening circles.)*

BLOSSOM
> *(singing)*

You spotted snakes with double tongue,
thorny hedgehogs, be not seen.
Newts and blindworms, do no wrong,
let sleep our Faerie Queen.

FAERIES
> *(singing)*

Lulla, lulla, lullaby; lulla, lulla, lullaby.
Sleep tight, sweet Lady, sleep sound.
Lulla, lulla, lullaby.

> *(Enter Oberon, unseen. As Faeries sing and dance, he sneaks to Titania.)*

MOTE
> *(singing)*

Weaving spiders, come not here.
Hence, you long-legged spinners, hence.
Beetles black, approach not here.
Worm nor snail, do no offense.

Act 2 Scene 6

FAERIES
(singing)
Lulla, lulla, lullaby; lulla, lulla, lullaby.
Sleep tight, sweet Lady, sleep sound.
Lulla, lulla, lullaby.

> *(Oberon takes out the magic flower and holds it high, over Titania.)*

COBWEB
(singing)
Goodnight, sweet Queen, goodnight.
Rest awhile, while we your faeries
make tomorrow's blooms bloom bright
before celebrating the morrow's merries.

FAERIES
(singing)
Lulla, lulla, lullaby; lulla, lulla, lullaby.
Sleep tight, sweet Lady, sleep sound.
Lulla, lulla, lullaby.

> *(Faeries exit.)*

OBERON
(touching the flower to her eyelids)
What thou seest when thou dost wake
do that for your true lover take.
When thou wak'st, it is thy dear.
And darling, I trust you shall

Wake when some vile thing is near.

> *(He rises and withdraws from Titania.)*

OBERON
I hope you wake to love a frog, or cat, or bear, mayhap a bug, even, that crawls upon your nose and wakes you to become your deepest love. Ha! This will teach you, oh stuck up high and mighty. You shall see. 'Tis not so easy when Cupid's arrow goes astray.

> *(He exits.)*

ACT 3

SCENE 1

Woods.

Titania and Thaddeus sleep unnoticed.

Enter Bottom, Quince, Stout, Starveling, Snug and Flute.

QUINCE
Come, players. Here is a marvelous convenient place for our rehearsal.

BOTTOM
Peter Quince?

QUINCE
What say you, weaver Bottom?

BOTTOM
There is a thing in this comedy of Pyramus and Thisbe that will never please. Pyramus must draw a sword to kill himself, which will fright the ladies. I shall, as custom dictates, wave a red handkerchief for blood, to please the men who insist on realism, but I fear the shock will fright

the fair. What say you?

QUINCE
No shock, for I will write you a prologue to warn that death and blood are coming.

BOTTOM
A prologue, yes! Give me many lines, for as a prologue comes before all else, it will be good for all to hear my voice first.

QUINCE
Your lines are first.

BOTTOM
Yes, but do write more.

STOUT
Will not the ladies be afeard of the lion?

STARVELING
I fear him, I promise you, after he's eaten his beans!

SNUG
Roar!

STOUT
Therefore, another prologue must tell he is not a real lion.

BOTTOM
Nay, let the lion but say his name, thus "Fair ladies, I would entreat you not to fear, not to tremble! I am a man as other men be, by name of Snug the joiner, your servant, all."

SNUG
F-f-fair la-la-la –

QUINCE
Fear not, Snug, just roar and let the ladies see your face. So long as you smile, they will not o'er tremble.

SNUG
(smiling)

Roar!

QUINCE
But in this script there are two hard things: that is, to bring moonlight into the chamber, for you know Pyramus and Thisbe meet by moonlight.

STOUT
Does the moon shine that night we play our play?

BOTTOM
A calendar, a calendar! Did no one bring an almanac? God's wounds, I work with amateurs!

STARVELING
I will run at once for a calendar! I go!

QUINCE
Hold! Masters, we are players, are we not? Let one of you come in with a bush of thorns and a lantern and say he comes to present the person of Moonshine. The second problem I find much harder: we must have a wall in the great chamber, for Pyramus and Thisbe, says the story, do talk through the chink of a wall.

FLUTE
We can build a wall, out of planks and stone. Is that in our budget?

SNUG
Bu-bu-budget?

FLUTE
(holding his hand out to Snug)
Have you paid your acting fee yet?

(Snug pays Flute.)

STOUT
You can never bring in a wall. What say you, Bottom?

BOTTOM
Some man or other must present Wall. And let him have some plaster, or some drywall and paint roughcast about him to signify wall, and let him stand thus, and through this cranny shall Pyramus

and Thisbe whisper.

QUINCE

If that may be, then all is well. These were the only difficulties I foresee in our script, and we may proceed.

SNUG

Roar!

QUINCE

Later, Snug. We begin with the prologue I shall write for Bottom -- Pyramus.

STOUT

And the one for Snug, to explain his lion is not the real and terrifying beast.

QUINCE

Yes, and that. We then begin our script. Masters, take places!

(They pose. Puck enters unseen.)

PUCK
(Aside.)

What hempen homespuns have we swagg'ring here? What, do they play a play of sorts? I'll be audience, and actor too perhaps, if I see cause for fun and games.

Act 3 Scene 1

QUINCE
Speak, Pyramus. For what do you wait?

BOTTOM
What cue shall I have that the prologue has finished? I must know my cue to begin timely.

QUINCE
It is finished when the words stop.

BOTTOM
Yes?

QUINCE
And then, you begin.

BOTTOM
Oh, Peter Quince. Far be it from me to tell you how to direct. But as I am focused on preparing myself in the lead role, perhaps if you, being then on stage too, idly standing by, may hold a finger up, thus, and drop it, thus, at the conclusion of the prologue, then will I have a visual cue as is done on the prouder professional stages I have trod.

QUINCE
Very well.

(Quince waves his finger pointedly.)

BOTTOM
Is that it? Are you going to do it like that?

PUCK
(Aside.)
What an ass is this fellow!

QUINCE
(waving his finger)
Begin, Bottom! Begin!

BOTTOM
(as Pyramus)
Thisbe, my dearest, the flowers savor sweet,
so is thy breath, my dearest Thisbe dear!
But hark, a voice! I must see who comes. Stay thou
but here awhile, and by and by I will to thee
reappear.

(He exits.)

PUCK
(Aside.)
This is my cue!

(Puck exits.)

FLUTE
Must I speak now?

QUINCE
Aye, marry, must you, for your lines are next.

Act 3 Scene 1

FLUTE
(as Thisbe)
Most radiant Pyramus, come back soon!
Look off for him, then seem to pine in sorrow.

QUINCE
Good day, man! You speak all your part at once,
cues and all. Speak not the action cues.

FLUTE
Oh!
(as Thisbe)
Good Pyramus, return to my side!

BOTTOM (O.S)
I do come now!

(Enter Puck, unseen.)

PUCK
(Aside.)
Here have I had some fun!

(Enter Bottom wearing a horse's head.)

BOTTOM (HORSEHEAD)
(as Pyramus)
Oh, fair Thisbe, I say with all due import
HEE-HAW!

(Puck runs at the players, barking.)

QUINCE
Oh, monstrous! Oh, strange! We are in haunted woods, bewitched! Fly, masters! Help!

(Quince, Flute, Stout, Snug and Starveling exit.)

PUCK
Ha ha! Such fools! Such fun!

(Barking again, Puck chases the players out.)

BOTTOM (HORSEHEAD)
Why do they – HEE-HAW! – run away?

(Quince re-enters.)

QUINCE
Bottom, can it be you? Bless you, poor man, you are translated! But hark! The hell hounds return!

(Puck re-enters and chases Quince, barking. They exit.)

BOTTOM (HORSEHEAD)
Hell hounds? I see no such, hear nothing. I see through their knavery. They are jealous.
This is to make an ass of me, if they could, to take

my lead from me. But I will not stir from
this place. I will – HEE-HAW! – walk up
and down here, and I will sing and dance, that
they shall hear I am not afraid.
                         (he sings and dances)
The ouzel cock, so black of hue,
with orange – HEW-HAW! – *tawny bill,*
and – HEE-HAW! – *stature true;*
the tiny wren – HEE-HAW! – *with little quill,*
HEE-HAW! HEE-HAW! HEE-HAW!

           TITANIA
                (waking up)
What angel's song wakes me from flow'ry bed?

           BOTTOM (HORSEHEAD)
                (singing)
HEE-HAW! HEE-HAW! – *and the lark,*
the plainsong cuckoo gray,
whose note full many a man doth –-
                (seeing Titania)
HEE-HAW!

           TITANIA
I pray thee, gentle mortal, sing again.
Mine ear is much enamored of thy note,
so is mine eye enthrallèd to thy shape.
and thy fair virtue's force doth move me
on the first view to say, to swear, I love thee.

           BOTTOM (HORSEHEAD)
Mistress, I have just begun. Rarely do the first

notes evoke such response, but I am willing to give autographs to my fans.

TITANIA
Thou art as wise as thou art beautiful.

BOTTOM (HORSEHEAD)
Yes, I am. – HEE-HAW! -- Perhaps, though, I should rejoin my friends.

TITANIA
Out of this wood do not desire to go.
Here is my love and everything you need.
And see, here is hay.

BOTTOM (HORSEHEAD)
(nibbling on the hay she holds)
Hay? Oh, this is good! – HEE-HAW! – How have I never known before how good is hay?

TITANIA
Here in the woods beside me you belong,
and I do love thee. Therefore go with me.

BOTTOM (HORSEHEAD)
But – HEE-HAW! -- this seems a dream. Did I not so long ago enter the woods with friends?

TITANIA
Here be all the friends you need. Peaseblossom, Cobweb, Mote, and Mustardseed!

Act 3 Scene 1

(Enter the Faeries.)

FAERIES
Ready! Here we are! Good morning, Lady Titania!

COBWEB
Oh! A mortal!

MUSTARD
Is it? It's like none such I've ever seen.

MOTE
What big ears it has!

BLOSSOM
Shall we drive this thing away, your Highness?

TITANIA
Be kind and courteous to this gentleman, my faeries. Treat him well and fair.
Bring him all he can eat and drink, for love him with all my heart I do.

COBWEB
Ma'am?

TITANIA
Hop in his walks and gambol in his eyes;
feed him with apricots and dewberries,
with purple grapes, green figs, and hay. Brush his mane and make him comfortable, so that he may lie about and have no worries but to be my love.

Act 3 Scene 1

MOTE
Hail, mortal!

BLOSSOM
Hail, I think?

MUSTARD
Hail! We are Cobweb, Blossom, Mote, and me, Mustardseed.

BOTTOM (HORSEHEAD)
HEE-HAW!

FAERIES
Oh!

TITANIA
Isn't he dear?

BOTTOM (HORSEHEAD)
I shall desire you of more acquaintance, good Masters Cobweb, Squash, Peabrain and Turd.

MUSTARD
What!

TITANIA
Those names are good as any. Come kiss me, my love.

COBWEB
(Aside.)
Something is wrong here. The air this morning has smell of mischief.

BOTTOM (HORSEHEAD)
HEE-HAW! HEE-HAW!

COBWEB
(Aside.)
Puck! This smells of Puck!

(Cobweb exits.)

TITANIA
Come, wait upon him. Lead him to my bower.

BOTTOM (HORSEHEAD)
HEE-HAW!

TITANIA
Tie up my lover's tongue. Bring him silently.

(Faeries and Bottom exit. Titania stops, seeing Thaddeus.)

TITANIA
Oh, my. I almost forgot this one. You there, Duke Thaddeus, wake and be off. You do not belong out here in the woods.

Act 3 Scene 1

(She claps her hands, and then exits.

Thaddeus awakes.)

THADDEUS
Oh, I must have dropped off. I'm still so tired. Where am I? I think I dreamed about faeries, of all things! As if faeries were real!

(Blossom enters unseen. She trips Thaddeus.)

THADDEUS
What now?

(Blossom laughs and exits.)

THADDEUS
It's like the trees do laugh at me. I must get out of these creepy woods and back to Athens!

(He exits.)

SCENE 2

Woods.

Oberon enters.

OBERON
Up ahead, coming this way, I hear someone as they approach. Invisible shall I be.

(Enter Breonna.)

BREONNA
For ages I've searched for him, that mystery man who years ago swept me off my feet. It was in a forest like this. I remember, I was minding my own business when of a sudden he stood there, like a Greek god just appearing out of nowhere. My eyes thought there was a glow around him, like he was magic or something! Oh, he was so fine! I looked at him and just said "ooooo" and next I knowed he was holding me, kissing me, touching me, and … ah, but then he left me alone, with child, and now he's gone. Again.

OBERON
(Aside.)
It is handy, being invisible.

(Oberon waves his arm, and Breonna yawns.)

Act 3 Scene 2

BREONNA
I must rest right here, awhile. I'm so tired!

(She sleeps.

Enter Philo with his net.

Philo pounces on a bush.)

PHILO
Gotcha! Oh, damn. Nothing.

(Enter Quince, Stout, Starveling and Snug running.)

QUINCE
Look out! Here come hell hounds!

PHILO
What?

(Enter Puck, barking. Chaos ensues as they all run in circles.

It ends when Philo nets Puck.

Puck stands, waves his arms, and the others freeze all movement.)

PUCK
Nuts! These mortals have all the sense of squirrels chasing nuts. So be it. This one with the net is the strangest, yet. He is a nut! Ha ha!

(Philo turns into a big acorn.)

PUCK
And these are hungry squirrels!

(The Players turn into squirrels.)

PUCK
Humans make good squirrels.

(Enter Thaddeus.)

THADDEUS
What goes on here? What is this noise and odd commotion?

PUCK
Here be another squirrel!

(Thaddeus turns into a squirrel.)

PUCK
Now, have at it, fools!

(The Players and Thaddeus all jump around, as squirrels. Philo stands shocked. The Squirrels turn to him.)

PHILO (NUT)

Am I a nut? And they, squirrels? Oh, no! They're going to eat me!

(He exits.)

PUCK

Go on, get the nut!

(Squirrels exit with chirping squirrel noises.)

PUCK

Ha ha ha ha!

(Oberon comes forward.)

OBERON

Ha! Well done, Robin. That bit with the nut was inspired!

PUCK

At your service, my king.

OBERON

Say, there is one you missed, right here. This one.

Act 3 Scene 2

PUCK
Another squirrel!

(Puck waves, and Breonna jumps up as a squirrel.)

PUCK
The Nut ran that way.

(Breonna exits.)

OBERON
Get this, Robin Goodfellow, the one you put the horse's head on, that is the one my dear Titania now loves!

PUCK
Ha ha ha! He is an ass!

OBERON
She thinks not. To her, that ass is the most handsomest love ever.

(Enter Hermia and Peter.)

OBERON
Hide. This is the same Athenian I told you of.

PUCK
This is the woman, but not this the man.

(They withdraw.)

Act 3 Scene 2

PETER
Oh, why do you rebuke him that loves you so?

HERMIA
I do not and will not ever love you, Peter.
If you have slain my Lyle in his sleep, I have
reason not just to not love but more to hate you.
Would he have stolen away from sleeping
Hermia?
I looked and found not him but you, sneaking
through the woods. It cannot be but that you have
murdered him. So should a murderer look, so
dead, so grim.

PETER
So should the murdered look, as do I. Pierced
through the heart with your stern cruelty.

HERMIA
What's this to my sweet Lyle? To your woodsy
strength and guile, he'd stand no chance. Ah,
tell me, where is he? Good Peter, will you give
him me?

PETER
I had rather give his carcass to my hounds.

HERMIA
Oh, no, do not say so! You are a cur, for
murdering my love! Never can you be again
numbered among men.

Act 3 Scene 2

PETER
Hold, rest your passion, sweet love. I am not guilty of Lyle's blood, nor is he dead, for aught I can tell.

HERMIA
I pray then, tell me is he well? Where is he?

PETER
Would I tell you for a kiss?

HERMIA
Fie on you! I hate you!

(She exits.)

PETER
There is no following her in this fierce vein.
Here, therefore, for a while I remain,
to sleep and rest some this night.

(He sleeps.)

OBERON
What have you done? Thou hast mistaken quite
and laid the love juice on some other's sight.
This is my son, whom I had trusted you to steer to the good graces of my wife's dear daughter.

PUCK
But, this man here does wear Athenian clothes!

Act 3 Scene 2

OBERON
Quick. About the woods fly you hence and bring here the daughter Helena, so that we can redo this bond.

PUCK
I go, I go, look how I go,
swifter than did Cupid's arrow first fly.

(He exits.)

OBERON
(applying flower juice to Peter's eyelids)
Flower, flower, do your job. Let this fair youth love the woman he wakes to see.

(Enter Puck.)

PUCK
Good King Oberon, the woods are full of people tonight. I had not gone far before finding Helena coming near.

OBERON
I hear them coming. Stand aside. Let us hope the noise they make will cause Peter to awake.

PUCK
Then will Peter love the one his glance first falls upon.

Act 3 Scene 2

(They withdraw.

Enter Lyle and Helen.)

LYLE
Why should you think that I should woo in scorn?

HELEN
You do advance your cunning more and more.
The oaths you swear of love and fealty are the
same you promised Hermia. Oh, inconstant man!

LYLE
My childhood with Hermia was pleasant, but my
heart has grown. You must see we are no longer
children. Helen, I see now, the love for me mature
is you.

HELEN
You are for Hermia. I cannot take her love.

LYLE
Peter loves her, and he loves not you. My god,
look here: sleeping upon the ground, it is Peter!

PUCK
(Aside to Oberon.)
Oh, watch. Ha ha! Peter will wake and first see
Lyle!

OBERON
(Aside to Puck.)
Stop him!

(Puck pushes Helen so that she falls in front of Peter.)

PETER
(waking up)
Oh, Helen -- goddess, nymph, perfect, divine!
To what, my love, shall I compare thine eyes?
Thy lip, those kissing cherries, tempting grow!
Oh, let me kiss this princess of pure bliss!

HELEN
Oh, spite! Oh, hell! I see you are all bent
to set against me for your merriment.
If you were civil and knew courtesy,
you would not do me this much injury.

LYLE
You are unkind, Peter. Be not so,
for you love Hermia; this you know I know.
And here with all goodwill, with all my heart,
I yield up to you all claim on Hermia's love.
Make her father the Duke happy, for you are free
to marry her. But in turn, release you Helen to me.

HELEN
Never did mockers waste more idle breath.

PETER
Lyle, keep you Hermia. Helen knows my love for

Hermia was always feigned, a feint crafted by my mother in hopes of ruling Athens. I went along only to make my mother happy, but I can do so no longer. Love trumps gold and power. My love for Helen is true.

(Enter Hermia.)

HERMIA
Ah, Lyle, my ears brought me to your sound. But why unkindly did you leave me so?

LYLE
Why should he stay whom love presses to go?

HERMIA
What love could press you from my side?

LYLE
My love for fair Helen, this gilded angel waiting patiently by.

HERMIA
You speak not as you think. It cannot be.

HELEN
You, too, Hermia? Have you conspired, have you with these contrived, to bait me with this foul derision?

HERMIA
I am amazed at your words.

I scorn you not. It seems that you scorn me.

HELEN

Have you not set Lyle, as in scorn,
to follow me and praise my eyes and face,
and made your other love, Peter,
who but moments ago did kick me away,
to call me goddess, nymph, divine and celestial?

HERMIA

I understand not what you mean by this.

HELEN

Fair Hermia, your whole life, you have been at every age the subject of desire. Well used to such praise you must be! But not I, and so my ears are critical and I see through this drivel. These empty words, these false proclamations of love, this fawning behavior is clearly false, as it cannot be directed at me.

PETER
(To Lyle.)

You have upset her!

LYLE

It is you who intervenes. Stick you with your Hermia.

PETER

Hermia? Her? Not another minute. You take her.

LYLE
I will not! Though I've had no breakfast, if I had it would be at risk of reappearing, just to think of being with her.

HERMIA
Do you not jest?

HELEN
Yes, he does, and so do you.

LYLE
Helen, come away with me.

HERMIA
What?

PETER
Lyle, you are distressing Helen. I must ask you to kindly retreat away from her. End your games and settle for Hermia.

HERMIA
Settle?

LYLE
Back off, Lyle. The Duke has chosen Hermia for you, and you for Hermia. Live long and prosper. Far away from Helen and I.

PETER
You push the wrong case, sir. Push not further or

you will force me to call you out.

LYLE
Your rude pressure troubles my lady, sir. Be gone, or draw your steel!

PETER
Steel it is!

(They jump up and draw their swords.)

HELEN
You go so far, to pretend now to duel over me?

HERMIA
Lyle! What are you doing?

(Hermia throws herself at Lyle and clings to him.)

HELEN
This is too much!

(Helen exits.)

HERMIA
Am I not Hermia? Are not you Lyle?
What woodsy tragedy has occurred, that you
in night did love me, and yet since night have left me?

(Peter exits, following Helen. Lyle struggles to get loose.)

LYLE
Aye, I am me, and you are you, and though hard to hear, 'tis no jest that I do hate thee and love Helen.

(Hermia turns him loose.)

HERMIA
What has she done to you? What trickery, what low and foul maneuvers? Now I perceive that she has cunningly laid a trap for me, to take not only all of Athens, which I freely left for her, but also the one single thing I prized above all else: your love.

LYLE
I must find her! If I must kill Peter, so be that, too.

(He exits.)

HERMIA
So do I hate Helen! I will kill her!

(She exits.)

OBERON
Well, that went well.

PUCK
Ha ha! Such fun! These mortals are silly fools –

OBERON
I spoke in sarcasm, Robin.

PUCK
Oh.

OBERON
These lovers are at each other's throats, for which we – especially you – share the blame.

PUCK
Is this not like the fun we had in Spain, turning bullfighters to love their bulls and with red capes and sharp swords chase their women? We both laughed then.

OBERON
Events have of late caused me to re-examine my ways, and I cannot feel good about this slaughter. Go, and make sure neither firebrand is able to hurt the other, while I search out the herb that counters Cupid's lovespell flower.

PUCK
My fairy lord, ever do I strive to please.

OBERON
Sarcasm?

PUCK
No, lord!

OBERON
Go, then, before steel finds blood.

> *(Oberon exits.*
>
> *Philo enters, screaming.)*

PHILO (NUT)
I am not a nut!

> *(Quince, Stout, Starveling, Snug, Thaddeus, and Breonna enter in chase, as Squirrels, making squirrel noises.)*

PHILO (NUT)
This shell is fake! I wouldn't taste good to any of you squirrely monsters!

> *(Philo and Squirrels exit.)*

PUCK
I'd forgotten about you weirdos. I wish I could play, and perhaps chase the Nut myself. Ah, but duty needs me.

> *(He calls out, mimicking voices.)*

Act 3 Scene 2

>   PUCK (PETER O.S.)
> Lyle, I am ready to duel! Come you this way! Hide not from me, you coward!
>
>   *(Enter Lyle.)*
>   LYLE
>   *(not seeing Puck)*
> Where are you, Peter? Speak now.
>
>   PUCK (PETER O.S.)
> Here, villain, drawn and ready, Where are you?
>
>   LYLE
> Ready!
>
>   PUCK (PETER O.S.)
> Follow me then to plainer ground.
>
>   *(Lyle exits.*
>
>   *Peter enters.)*
>
>   PETER
> Lyle, speak again. You runaway coward, are you again fled? Speak! In some bush? Behind some tree?
>
>   PUCK (LYLE O.S.)
> Follow my voice. We'll try no manhood here.
>
>   *(Puck and Peter exit.*

Lyle enters.)

LYLE
He goes before me and still dares me on.
When I come where he calls, then he is gone.
The villain is much lighter-heeled than I.
I will rest, 'til come the gentle day.

(He sleeps.

Enter Puck waving branches in front of Peter.)

PETER
You run ever before me, so close, but all I catch are glimpses of moving trees and bushes. This duel will be better concluded in daylight, for I am too tired to put up with your tomfoolery.

(He sleeps.)

PUCK (HELEN O.S.)
Oh, Hermia, come this way. We will have this out, the two of us, woman to woman.

(Hermia enters.)

HERMIA
I've been chasing all over to reach you! Are you here? I swear, I just heard that girl. Why do try? I forget she is at home in the woods, not I. This will all work out in the light. Now, I sleep.

Act 3 Scene 2

(She sleeps.)

PUCK
Yet but three? Come one more.
Two of both kinds makes up four.
Here she comes, curst and sad.
Cupid is a knavish lad
thus to make poor females mad.

(Enter Helen.)

HELEN
The world has all gone bonkers. These friends I thought I knew strive to make me crazy. I am better off staying in the woods, and may just do so. I can live happily, by myself, with none other to hurt me. Tomorrow's plan that is. Yet for the rest of this night, I will sleep now here.

(She sleeps.

Philo enters.)

PHILO (NUT)
Help! Somebody, help!

(Puck waves his arm, and Philo freezes all movement.)

PUCK
Stay, King Nut, or you will undo my hard work and awake these lovers before I am done.

(The Squirrels enter noisily, until Puck causes them to freeze, also.)

PUCK
All of you, lay down and sleep!

(They sleep.)

PUCK
What a night!

(Puck drags Peter near Helen, and turns Peter's head to look at her.)

PUCK
(waving the lovespell flower)
Here is correct love for you.

(He drags Lyle near Hermia, and positions their heads.)

PUCK
(waving the lovespell flower)
And you, for you. You lovers now lie properly aligned; let none of you roll over in your sleep. Hermia and Lyle shall see each other, and my king's half son, Peter, shall wake to see Queen Titania's half daughter.

(Enter Cobweb.)

Act 3 Scene 2

COBWEB

Hey, honey. I see you are busy. I knew these happenings tonight arose through your mischief. Are those the lovespell flowers?

PUCK

Aye, yes, and this the plant, too, the herb to reverse love's spell. Both from my king, good Oberon.

COBWEB

Are you through here? Perchance, there is a place where you and I might speak more of this, where can intrude no mortal ears, asleep or not?

PUCK

Most certainly!

(They exit.)

ACT 4

SCENE 1

Woods.

With Lovers, Nut and Squirrels still asleep.

Titania, Blossom, Mote, Mustard, and Bottom enter.

Oberon enters, unseen.

BLOSSOM
My Lady! There are many mortals asleep in the woods!

TITANIA
But find a pleasant spot for Bottom Horsehead and I to lay, for I care not about other sleepers.

BLOSSOM
Okay ….

(The Faeries create a bed place.)

Act 4 Scene 1

> BOTTOM (HORSEHEAD)
> It sure must be late. I feel – HEE-HAW! – as if I've been up all night.

> TITANIA
> Come rest, my love.

> BOTTOM (HORSEHEAD)
> Is this a soft spot? I am such a tender ass.

> TITANIA
> Will you hear some music, my sweet love?

> BOTTOM (HORSEHEAD)
> Later, perhaps. How about some more hay now?

> TITANIA
> Of course!

(Faeries bring hay.)

> BOTTOM (HORSEHEAD)
> *(eating hay)*
> I will forever remember this night as the time I learned how good is hay. MMMM – HEE-HAW! HEE-HAW! Wow, this stuff is delicious! I'll save this bunch for the morn. I do admit to feeling drowsy.

> TITANIA
> Sleep, love, and I will wind you in my arms. Faeries, begone, and give us this night.

Act 4 Scene 1

>   *(Faeries exit.)*

BOTTOM (HORSEHEAD)
>   *(falling asleep)*

HEE-haaaaaaw.

TITANIA

Oh, you are the cutest thing. How I dote on you!

>   *(She sleeps.*
>
>   *Oberon comes forward.)*

OBERON

What a sweet sight. My wife, I do begin to pity you, under love's control.
We long have quarreled over our mortal loves, me with Lady Breonna, and you the Duke.
I wish you could have seen that my dalliance meant nothing but a momentary release,
while you have committed the greater foul watching years over your mortal playthings.
Still, I do now repent, and wish I could undo the harm done, the tears my straying has brought to your eyes.
This lovespell trick was meant to teach you a lesson, and yet it is I who feel taught and humbled.

>   *(Titania rises.)*

Act 4 Scene 1

TITANIA
Good! And about time, you buzzard. This game of pretending to love the ass was growing stale.

OBERON
What? Are you not under spell?

TITANIA
Heavens no, dear heart, though not for lack of your trying. My faerie Cobweb saw through the ruse and brought me the countering herb, stolen from your Puck.

OBERON
Why, what a sneak! And so you but pretended to let me have my moment, huh?

TITANIA
Hoping that you might learn what you have learned, and happy now to call you husband.

OBERON
Wife.

TITANIA
Faeries!

OBERON
Puck!

(Blossom, Mote and Mustard enter.)

FAERIES
My queen?

(Puck enters.)

PUCK
My king?

(Cobweb enters, looking sheepish.)

COBWEB
My Queen? Sire?

(Oberon looks sternly at Cobweb, then grins.)

TITANIA
Faeries, now is our feud with husband king over. I lift all restrictions on your ways. Let the faerie world be once again united!

OBERON
Shall we return to our realm, or stay the day to watch the wedding celebration?

TITANIA
Let us stay and renew our own vows, even as the mortals do.

OBERON
How romantic.

Act 4 Scene 1

(He kisses Titania.)

FAERIES
Ahhh!

PUCK
My good king, uh, sir. What of all these?

OBERON
Good Puck, do remove that beastly horse head and let these all return to their wits, with the dawning light. Oh, but one thing, just to be sure.

(Oberon turns Breonna's head to look at Thaddeus, and waves the lovespell flowers over her eyelids.)

OBERON
These flowers will help you feel what you already profess to feel, and for love not money.

(Oberon, Titania, Blossom, Mote, and Mustard exit.)

COBWEB
I'd like to stay and help you, Robin.

PUCK
Lend me your magic then, for there are many. Let us de-ass the ass, first.

> *(Puck and Cobweb wave their arms over Bottom Horsehead.)*

PUCK / COBWEB
Awake!

> *(Bottom wakes, without his horsehead.)*

BOTTOM
When my cue comes, call me, and I will be ready! What? Oh, but what a dream I was having! I will get Peter Quince to write a ballad of this dream. It shall be called "Bottom's Dream" because it has no bottom, and I will sing it in the latter end of a play before the Duke.

> *(Puck and Cobweb wave and the other Players awake, as themselves.)*

BOTTOM
Get up, Quince, lazy bones. We must write a play, for I have had an adventure!

QUINCE
But, did we fall asleep in rehearsal?

SNUG
I th-th-thought I was a squirrel, not lion.

STOUT
Me, too! I have an intense craving for nuts!

QUINCE
Quiet, there are others here who may hear our plans. Let us pull back to where we can rehearse unseen.

STARVELING
It is morn already. We've got only a few hours to ready ourselves to play our scene before the Duke.

BOTTOM
Come, then! Stop lounging about!

(Players exit.)

PUCK
And now, the rest.

(He and Cobweb wave. The Lovers, Thaddeus and Breonna, and Philo all awake.)

PHILO
(Seeing Lyle.)
Ah ha! I knew I'd find you! There is still time to get you to your ship, young sailor to be!

(Philo leaps and wraps his arms around Lyle.)

Act 4 Scene 1

HERMIA
No, let him go!

THADDEUS
Good Philo, halt your efforts.

(Philo releases Lyle.)

THADDEUS
How came we all here, to wake together? I have no memory of this midsummer's night, but for strange and wondrous dreams clouding my mind. Hermia, you stand close with Lyle. Helen, you close with Peter. See you this, dear Breonna? These are not four persons, but clearly two couples in love.

(Breonna hugs Thaddeus.)

BREONNA
Not two, but three loving couples, my love.

THADDEUS
Good morning!

BREONNA
It is. This is our wedding day.

THADDEUS
Let it be the wedding day for all three couples!

(The Lovers kiss.)

Act 4 Scene 1

PHILO

Oh my god, my lord, see how high the sun has too fast risen! We are much behind schedule, and yet deep in the woods! We must be off, in a rush-rush hurry, to make this day count as planned.

THADDEUS

Relax, Philo. I am Duke, so I make the rules, remember? The wedding celebrations shall start when I say so. Come, all. Join me on the palace grounds where by now must wait the nobles and the necessary friar.

LYLE

(kneeling)

Hermia?

(Helen kneels to ask the same question of Peter, but he pulls her up, and himself kneels before her.)

PETER

Helen?

HERMIA / HELEN

Yes!

BREONNA

Come, for we have prepared the finest foods, and also set up much entertainment for our receptions.

Act 4 Scene 1

PHILO
Oh, yes, ma'am! Dancing pigs; a eunuch who sings while playing harp; one small girl who juggles ice cream cones, without dropping a drop, and another who milks her cow with bells upon the udders; and some of the best players for scenes of love and bravery and frightful action.

(Lovers and Philo exit.)

COBWEB
We can join the others, to watch the mortal games. Or, I do know of a friendly spot by the lake, in which we could dilly dally before rejoining?

PUCK
Dilly dally it is!

(They exit.)

ACT 5

SCENE 1

Palace grounds.

Enter Thaddeus & Breonna, Hermia & Lyle, Helen & Peter, arm in arm, with Philo, nobles, and attendants.

THADDEUS
Enough wine and dance, let us now sit again for more entertainment! Sweet Hermia, what has been your favorite act, so far?

HERMIA
I think, the one-legged unicyclist playing violin. The way he hopped on high note, how I loved it!

HELEN
My favorite has been the singing 'possums.

LYLE
Oh, but they just whined, not true singing. The parrot from southern isles, though, oh that parrot could really sing!

Act 5 Scene 1

PETER
Too bad it knew only "*hello,*" "*give me a cracker*" and "*someone feed the cat.*"

BREONNA
Oh, how wonderful this day has been!

THADDEUS
Not over, yet, dear heart, and believe me, I am counting the minutes until it is just you and I in my room – our room – above.

BREONNA
You tiger!

HERMIA
Ahem, what's next, father?

THADDEUS
Philo?

PHILO
Yes, well you'll be glad to know that while you took refreshment, we cleaned the stage and all the area about your seats. No sign remains of Sven and his dancing pigs.

PETER
Crapping pigs! Ha ha!

PHILO
Now come local players, tradesmen of Athens by

day, to give us, uh, the "Tedious brief scene of young Pyramus and his love Thisbe, very magical mirth, with no real lion." They say brief, for it is short, but time enough for Pyramus therein to kill himself.

THADDEUS
Oh, sounds good.

PHILO
No, my lord, not, I fear. At least not in rehearsal.

THADDEUS
We will hear it. Take your places, ladies.

(Philo exits. All sit.

Philo re-enters.)

PHILO
So please your grace, the Prologue is addressed.

THADDEUS
Let him approach.

(Bottom enters.)

BOTTOM
Forthwith upon this stage
shall we present and you shall see
the story of Pyramus – played by me, Bottom the weaver, uh, Bottom the Star – and his love Thisbe.

Let's see – oh, yes. Have no fear, ladies, when a lion appears, for I tell you now the lion is not real. And, too, please don't faint when I die, for I do not.

(He exits.)

THADDEUS
Good prologue. He is a weaver; I have several of his blankets, and – oh, but excuse me!

LYLE
Yes, he is my father. I have not yet seen him all day long, and have had no time to tell him of the wedding.

HERMIA
Well, good thing he was planning on coming anyway! I will meet him after the scene concludes.

(Enter Pyramus (Bottom), Thisbe (Flute), Wall (Stout), Moonshine (Starveling), Lion (Snug) and Quince.)

QUINCE
Gentles, perchance you wonder at this show. This man with lime and roughcast plaster does present "Wall", that vile wall which did separate our lovers and through Wall's chink, poor souls, they must be content to whisper.
This man with lantern and bush of thorn presents

"Moonshine," for by moonshine did these lovers woo.
And this grisly beast is called "Lion," the ferocious – but don't worry, not real! – untamed jungle cat that does scare the trusty Thisbe almost to death. We begin!

(Snug, Flute, Starveling and Quince withdraw.)

STOUT (WALL)
I, one Stout the tinker, present "Wall";
and such a wall as I would have you think
that had in it a crannied hole or chink
through which the lovers, Pyramus and Thisbe,
did whisper often.

THADDEUS
A good wall, surely. Stout, with a chink.

PETER
It is the wittiest partition that ever I heard discourse, my lord.

(Quince comes forward to cue Bottom with his finger, then withdraws.)

BOTTOM (PYRAMUS)
Oh, grim-looking night! Oh, night, which ever art when day is not! Oh, night! Oh, night!
Alas, I fear my Thisbe's promise is forgot.

Here is night, here is Wall, and here is Chink,
but what see I? No Thisbe do I see.

          THADDEUS
The wall, methinks, being sensible, should curse
the night again.

          BOTTOM
No, in truth, sir, he should not. "No Thisbe do I
see" is Thisbe's cue. He is – I mean, apologies my
lord, she is to enter now, and I am to espy her
through this wall.
                     (whispered)
Now, Flute!

                 (Flute comes forward.)

        FLUTE (THISBE)
Oh, Wall, full often have you heard my moans
for parting my fair Pyramus and me.
My cherry lips have oft kissed your stones
while the --

        BOTTOM (PYRAMUS)
I see a voice! Thisbe, is that my love?

           FLUTE
                     (whispered)
You didn't let me finish, Bottom!

        FLUTE (THISBE)
My love! Thou art my love, I think.

BOTTOM (PYRAMUS)
Oh, kiss me though the hole of this vile wall.

(They attempt to kiss.)

BOTTOM (PYRAMUS)
Push your lips harder, dear.

FLUTE (THISBE)
I kiss the wall's hole, not your lips at all.

BOTTOM (PYRAMUS)
Wilt thou at Ninny's tomb meet me straightway?

FLUTE (THISBE)
I go without delay.

(Bottom and Flute withdraw.)

STOUT (WALL)
Thus have I my part discharged.

(He withdraws.)

HERMIA
This is the silliest stuff that ever I heard!

THADDEUS
Even bad plays are good, if imagination amend them.

BREONNA
It must be your imagination then, not theirs.

THADDEUS
If we imagine no worse of them than they of themselves, they may pass for excellent men. Here comes the beast.

> *(Snug and Starveling come forward.)*

SNUG
La-la-ladies, do not fear. I-I am re-re-really just Snug the joiner.

HELEN
What's a joiner?

LYLE
A woodworker. A carpenter. Snug works in the stable next to my father's place.

SNUG
Hi, Lyle!

LYLE
Hi, Snug!

SNUG (LION)
Uh. Uh. To c-c-continue: Roar! Roar!

STARVELING (MOONSHINE)
This lantern doth the hornèd moon present.
Myself, the man in the moon.

THADDEUS
This seems in great error. The man should be put into the lantern. How else is it "man in the moon"?

PETER
He dare not climb in, for the candle would snuff.

LYLE
Proceed, Moon.

STARVELING
That's it Lyle. All that I have to say is that this lantern is moon, and I the man in the moon.

HERMIA
That is said then.

HELEN
What else is there?

STARVELING
(whispered)
Flute, move in!

(Flute comes forward.)

FLUTE (THISBE)
This is old Ninny's tomb. Where is my love?

Act 5 Scene 1

SNUG (LION)
Roar! ROAR!

(Snug attacks Flute, who drops a scarf and runs off.)

LYLE
Well roared, Lion!

HERMIA
Well run, Thisbe.

BREONNA
Well shone, Moon.

(Snug grabs the scarf and worries it.)

SNUG (LION)
Roar, roar, roar!

THADDEUS
Well worried, Lion. I can see the bloody scene in my mind.

SNUG
Th-th-thank you.

(Snug withdraws.

Bottom comes forward.)

Act 5 Scene 1

>PETER
>And then comes Pyramus.

>LYLE
>Must be why Lion vanished.

>BOTTOM (PYRAMUS)
>Sweet Moon, I thank thee for thy sunny beams
>which lead me to this place and show me – oh!
>But what is this?

>>*(He picks up the scarf, along with a red scarf hidden in his hand, lifting up both to be seen.)*

>BOTTOM (PYRAMUS)
>Oh, dainty duck! My Thisbe's mantel –
>what, stained with blood?
>Oh, wherefore, Nature, didst thou lions frame,
>since lion vile hath here deflowered my dear?
>Oh, vile world! Capricious nature!
>Out, sword, and wound me heart
>where heart is already dying dead.

>>*(He stabs himself, showing another red scarf.)*

>BOTTOM (PYRAMUS)
>Thus die I, thus, thus.
>Now am I dead;
>my soul is in the sky!

Act 5 Scene 1

Moon, take thy flight, for
my eyes have closed forever.

(Starveling withdraws.)

BREONNA
Does the moon then set upon a person's death?

THADDEUS
With eyes closed it may not be seen. We thus
experience the death ourselves.

BREONNA
A dead audience cannot be good for coin.

BOTTOM (PYRAMUS)
I die! I die! Oh, swordcut heart, let loose your
blood. Thus, with heavy heart no more pumping, I
die!

PETER
No die, but an ace for this fellow.

LYLE
He does well, does he not? My father
took first place last year on Wagon Day.

HERMIA
No! Really?

LYLE
Well done, father!

Act 5 Scene 1

BOTTOM
(jumping up upon hearing Lyle)
Lyle! My son, why sit you with the quality? You will be found out and hung!

(Bottom grabs Lyle to drag him off. Hermia grabs Lyle and pulls the other way.)

HERMIA
No, father! He stays with me!

BOTTOM
Why call you me "father"? Let loose, girl!

QUINCE
(running in)
Bottom, whatever are you at?

STARVELING
(joining Quince)
We'll all be hung, sure!

STOUT
Snug, distract the audience, while we grab Bottom and run.

(Snug runs forward, in front of Thaddeus.)

SNUG (LION)
Roar!

(Stout, Quince and Starveling attempt to pull Bottom loose. Peter and Helen join the fray to help Hermia pull Lyle.)

SNUG (LION)
ROAR! N-n-nothing to see here, my lord! Just a lion. ROAR!

THADDEUS
Good Masters, good Players all. Cease! Cease and listen to my decision!

BOTTOM
Run, Lyle!

LYLE
Father, no! Listen to the good Duke.

PHILO
I have him, my lord!

(Philo tackles Bottom, and they fall in a heap.)

THADDEUS
Thank you, Philo, that'll do. Good sir, Bottom the weaver, Star of this fine show, know you that this

day not two hours hence your son is my own; my daughter is your daughter. I happily call you family.

LYLE
Father, it's true. Meet my bride, your daughter, Hermia.

HERMIA
Well met, father.

BOTTOM
What? Lyle, married? To quality? I, the Duke's brother in law? That makes me Dukelet, or some such thing, yes?

BREONNA
Ha ha! It does not so work, good player.

THADDEUS
But good Bottom, perhaps another title may be bestowed. Philo, what acts have we yet to see?

PHILO
But two, my lord. A full set of trained jumping fleas, and a man with three nipples who makes his bellybutton sing.

HERMIA
Ewww.

Act 5 Scene 1

THADDEUS
I think, then, good Philo, we may pronounce the winners of today's contest: this band of merry tradesmen who put on such fine show of roaring lion, stout wall, beamy moonshine, and lovers dear.

STARVELING
We weren't done.

THADDEUS
Should we continue and see if this debacle is yet bested by a singing bellybutton?

QUINCE
We shall not keep your lordship from the feast which waits.
    (to the Players)
Come, present yourselves!

(The Players bow, and the audience claps for them.)

QUINCE
And the pay?

PHILO
Quiet, player.

THADDEUS
No, he is right. Good sir, did you write and direct this farce?

Act 5 Scene 1

QUINCE
Aye, sir.

THADDEUS
Then I pay your patience as much your skill, for this was as bad as bad could be, which sparked the imagination in me.

HELEN
It was funny.

HERMIA
So bad, that it was funny.

QUINCE
We try, madam.

THADDEUS
Here, good sir, is your gold-filled purse.

QUINCE
Thank you, lord Duke and Duchess!

BOTTOM
That makes us the best, then? And I am first, again?

THADDEUS
You, brother, I crown best clown of clowns.

BOTTOM
Yes! I am the best!

Act 5 Scene 1

THADDEUS
Good night, good sirs.

(The Players exit backwards, bowing.)

BREONNA
I'm for more refreshments. Anyone care to join?

THADDEUS
Capital idea.

HELEN
Are there more shrimp?

THADDEUS
Come, let us find out.

(They exit.

A mist forms, and Cobweb, Mote, Blossom and Mustard dance in.)

FAERIES
(singing)
Bells and cockleshells,
ring the shores of placid lakes
where Peace Harmony takes
to close this day that followed night
with love times three, and all is right.

Act 5 Scene 1

>(Enter Oberon, Titania, and Puck.)

TITANIA
All is right, and all shall be well, both
here with the mortals and so too the faeries.

OBERON
Let us magical folk leave mortals here
to continue our party in the forest, dear.
Through the woods give glimmering light,
by faerie dust and mystical fires.
Every elf and faerie sprite
shall attend in finest attires.

BLOSSOM
Yes, a party!

TITANIA
My good King Oberon, this day is much
for celebration, and I have one more gift
for you. 'Tis a gift you've well earned
which I pray you receive with dignity.

>(Titania waves, and a small child enters, wearing a horse's head.)

LITTLE HORSEHEAD
Hee-haw! Hee-haw!

TITANIA
Isn't he so cute!

OBERON
A gift I deserve, indeed. Welcome, uh –

TITANIA
I call him Cheeks.

(They exit, all but Puck.)

PUCK
(coming forward)
If we shadows have offended,
think but this and all is mended:
that you have but slumbered here
while these visions did appear.
And this weak and idle theme,
no more yielding but a dream.
Gentles, do not reprehend;
if you pardon, we will mend.
And, as I am an honest Puck,
if we have unearnèd luck
now to 'scape the serpent's tongue,
we will make amends ere long.
Else the Puck a liar call!

(Enter Cobweb, joining him.)

PUCK / COBWEB
So, good night unto you all!
Give us your hands, if we be friends,

and we shall restore amends.

(They exit.)

(CURTAINS.)

Key Changes from Shakespeare's play

This *Doable Midsummer Night's Dream* is very different from the original. More than others in the series to date, this is a complete re-write. As with all of the *Doable Shakespeare* series, the language has been altered to better fit modern ears; passages that seemed overly "artsy" or "poetic" were cut down; the order of the scenes and action has been tinkered with; and minor characters have either been given more lines, or else cut entirely, because every part should be fun to perform. As for specific changes to this play:

1. Shakespeare began this play by footing it in Greek mythology. Theseus and Hippolyta (Queen of the Amazons) were well known mythological figures. Theseus and other Greek heroes fought a war against the Amazons, and after Theseus defeated Hippolyta in battle, he took her to be his wife. Shakespeare's audience would know this background mythology, more so than modern audiences, so Shakespeare doesn't have to retell the story. He barely mentions it once. Today, we would have to retell the whole story, or else skip it altogether -- so out it goes. Then, since the names need no longer refer to Greek mythology, I changed the Duke's name to Thaddeus and her name to Breonna.

2. Tossing aside the mythology leaves us free to

invent, and at the same time build more rationalization for why Duke Thaddeus and Breonna care about what happens to four lovers sneaking off into the woods. In the original, Hermia's father, Egeus, comes to the Duke and begs the Duke to support his claim as to which boy Hermia should wed. The Duke and Duchess-to-be are seen in Act 1, and then appear at the end to support the couples getting married, but they are barely more than throw-away characters. By making Duke Thaddeus Hermia's father, and Breonna the mother of Peter, they are better motivated.

3. Similarly, the Faerie King and Queen are aloof characters who don't do much in the original. They do much more here! Originally, their argument stemmed from Oberon wanting a changeling boy who Titania refused to give him. That boy is a wasted character, barely referred to or used at all – so he's gone. Arguing over the boy was weak motivation for Titania to shun her husband, or for Oberon's vengeful prank on his wife. By connecting their argument to their past indiscretions with mortals, themes of love, cheating and revenge can be explored. Jealousy is a fine motivation, better by far than arguing over a meaningless boy.

4. Originally, Oberon uses the lovespell flowers to make Titania love Bottom, and she does so.

When Oberon undoes the effect, she goes meekly to her husband and asks him to tell her how she ended up with Bottom. The idea of a man drugging his wife into submission falls flat in today's world. Here, Oberon tries to do so, but Titania turns it around and gets Oberon to change. Her "gift" of Cheeks is a reminder that Oberon needs: that one lives with the consequences of one's actions.

5. The lovers are four separate people, in the original, with nothing tying them to other characters. Here, Hermia is the Duke's heir. Lyle is the base-born son of Bottom, the local rug weaver. Helen is the Duke's wild daughter from Queen Titania, and Peter is Breonna's son from her fling with King Oberon. That makes Helen and Peter demi-gods, essentially, though they have no superpowers to show for it – just a shared love of the woods, and perhaps ability to talk to bees.

6. Puck is mostly the same, and it is he that audiences tend to think of first when remembering *MSND*. But, surprisingly, in the original it isn't until Act 2 before Puck even appears, and he has a much smaller role than here. In this version, he opens the play, which seems especially fitting since Shakespeare has him giving the final good-bye speech to the audience.

7. Speaking of faeries, in the original they don't appear until Act 2, either. That seems odd, given that this play has always been about magic. The entire first act is pure exposition, the telling of which is (for me and others I know) boring and likely to put audiences to sleep. Here, the faeries are moved up. Also, their roles are fleshed out more so than in the original, Cobweb especially. All roles in a play should be fun to perform!

8. Bottom is as much an ass in the original, but one which waxes poetic to the point of somnolence. He is a selfish ass here, too, but hopefully a funnier clown. By making him also the father of Lyle, he has a stake in the outcome, and we can touch on the theme of Lyle moving up beyond his (father's) station.

9. The other players are, in the original, little more than people for Bottom to play off of. Personally, I find the original clown parts tiresome. Each role is more fun, here. Likewise, Philo (Philostrate) in the original has barely any presence, but here is a much more fun role to perform; here, Philo is one of the clowns. The whole squirrel-chasing-nut scene is freshly invented.

10. Speaking of clowns, their comic-relief use is built up throughout the play, but the play-

within-the-play device in Act 5 is considerably shortened. It might be that Shakespeare's audiences would have enjoyed the clowns' play, but to me the original scene seems to drag on forever.

11. And, of course, Cheeks is a brand new character. Generally, these *Doable Shakespeare* adaptations do away with characters that appear in only one scene; Cheeks is an exception. It is, however, a role that can be easily skipped, if your production so chooses or doesn't have access to a small boy or girl to play it.

Character Notes

You've been cast! Hoorah! Now, before fame and glory, roses and chocolate, steak and cast parties, you must get to work. *A Midsummer Night's Dream* is perhaps Shakespeare's simplest play; it is a lighthearted, silly comedy, with elements of romance, and should be presented with almost manic energy.

As is always the case with Shakespeare, even the smallest of roles is imbued with heart and intellect. The following character notes are meant as a starting point, to help you understand your character. Find what you can here, and then look elsewhere, everywhere, even inside yourself, to find more. Find and use anything, everything, that can help you bring these fun characters to life.

PUCK – The lovable, mischievous, powerful, supernatural creature. "Puck" is what he is, meaning a type of elf or goblin that would have been familiar to 16th century audiences; today, we'd be more likely to blame a poltergeist for weird things that happen around the house. "Puck" is not his name; it's Robin Goodfellow. However, most people just call him Puck. As with many things in the *Doable Shakespeare* series, we go with the easiest name.

Puck is a jester, a fun-loving prankster. He uses magic to play practical jokes, but in a harmless way. In *MSND*, Bottom and the other Players are the clowns that serve as comic relief, but Puck is the faerie world counterpart. He jokes directly with the audience, breaking the fourth wall in his speeches at the start and end of the play.

Puck moves the story along more than any other character. He puts the horse head on Bottom, turns Philo into a nut, and turns the Players, Breonna, and Thaddeus into squirrels. He chases the Players as if he were a hell hound. By mistakenly anointing Lyle's eyelids with the love potion, instead of Peter's, he creates chaos for the Lovers. He then confuses the Lovers, as Lyle and Peter threaten to duel.

He is capricious, full of magical fancy, and loves to mess with people just because he finds it funny how easy it is to fool mortals. He himself says no one is safe from his sharp eye. But like a poltergeist, his pranking is more fun than cruel. He has a kind heart, and promises in the end that he will "make amends" if anyone is offended.

Note that I've used the male pronoun for Puck, but there is no reason Puck could not be female. The name Robin is androgynous. (So, too, with the faeries.)

COBWEB

Though sweet and loving, as a faerie should be, Cobweb is the female counterpart to Puck. She is mischievous and sneaky, for a faerie. She serves her queen, but is willing to go against the queen's orders to slip away to see Puck. She has a clever intellect, and recognizes when Queen Titania is under the influence of Oberon's lovespell flowers; then she's sneaky enough to steal the antidote from Puck and save her queen.

Like Puck, Cobweb breaks the 4th wall at the end. She has an awareness greater than the stage.

BLOSSOM, MOTE and MUSTARD

These faeries are what all faeries should be: sweet, loving, wide-eyed, friendly, and ever ready to jump into song and dance.

Not stupid, naïve, or prudish – note Blossom's reaction when Puck hits on them, calling him a "naughty boy." They would be happy to meet with Puck and the rest of the faerie king's men, if their queen had not forbidden it. But these three are loyal followers of the

Queen and would never sneak off, like Cobweb.

The lines said together by the Faeries may be done in different ways – that's up to you and your director. The lines may be sung together, or maybe you'd rather divide the lines up between you, with one faerie finishing the other's start.

Faeries are magical creatures. On stage that is best portrayed through movement. Faeries should flit about, with a great amount of joyous energy. They should dance beautifully. They should spread joy and love – which can be indicated a number of ways, perhaps through lighting and sound cues, perhaps by throwing glitter ("faerie dust"), perhaps by plants or other items coming to life.

TITANIA – Queen of the Faeries, and very much a true and proper faerie, both sweet and loving. But Titania is royal, too, and she rules with a firm hand.

She flirts and has her own mischievous side, willing to prank her husband and tease mortals. She has withheld sex from her husband, and forbade her faeries from entertaining the king's men, in order to teach her husband a lesson. She pretends to love Bottom even after the love potion is countered, so that she can see if her husband has learned anything.

Titania has a fiery disposition, quick to temper. Not someone to be messed with!

Apparently, birth in the faerie world works

differently than with us humans. In the backstory, Duke Thaddeus and Titania met in the woods, and the resulting daughter is given to Thaddeus to raise. But no, this does not mean Thaddeus and Titania were dating for nine months of pregnancy; Titania was able to give Helen to him right away. Similarly, she is able to give Cheeks to Oberon. Don't get hung up over biology – this is faerie magic we're talking about here!

OBERON – King, and king in all respects, good with bad. He is a deep, conflicted character. Like many a human king in antiquity, he feels free to follow his lust-filled instincts, bedding whomever whenever and wherever opportunity lies. He sees nothing wrong with this, nor does he see any reason to care what happens afterwards.

He and his wife, Titania, long ago argued about their marital infidelities, an argument which has kept them apart for many years. He sees Titania's care for mortals as her weakness, but comes to feel guilt and chagrin at having abandoned his son, Peter.

He does redeem himself, by realizing responsibility comes with his actions.

THADDEUS – Duke of Athens, he is a fine ruler. All of Athens loves him, and so his pending wedding day is a big item for the town. The "event of the season" per Philo.

He was married before, and had a daughter with his first wife. What happened to that wife is not stated, but she's been gone so long that Hermia doesn't remember her. Perhaps this is why Thaddeus is so horny.

He is a total horn dog throughout the play. Driven by his lust, so much so that he is willing to force his daughter to marry Peter rather than risk Breonna leaving town.

He is also the voice of authority, willing to punish his own daughter if she doesn't submit to Athenian law.

BREONNA – Though loving at the end, it is fair to say that Breonna at first is a gold-digger. She has lived a hard life. Her first marriage ended with the death of her husband, and when she went into the woods King Oberon took advantage of her grief to impregnate her. She was happy to have a son, but her road was not easy as a single mother. Apparently, she and Peter had little to eat other than dried potatoes. Now, having met and successfully seduced the Duke, she sees the chance to turn her fortunes around.

She pressures Peter to marry Hermia, as another means to cement her hold on the Duke.

She withholds sex from Thaddeus, like a carrot held in front of a starving rabbit, but then falls all over Oberon. This show she is not prudish and has a strong sex drive herself, and will be a good match for the Duke.

HERMIA – The Duke's daughter with his first wife, and his stated heir. She is loved by all of Athens.

Sweet and loving by nature, fond of girly dresses and ready to someday take over after her father to lead Athens.

While a dutiful daughter, she is also strong enough to be her own person. It never occurred to her that Lyle needed to ask her father before they could court or become engaged. Though a father's right to decide for his daughter is said to be Athens' law, Hermia has missed that point or dismissed it. When her father insists she wed Peter, she chooses instead to become a nun or run away.

Love is stronger than duty, stronger than tradition, stronger than law. True love survives all challenges. Hermia's message is strong, and she more than anyone else is the protagonist of the play.

HELEN – The Duke's second daughter, though raised as his ward since she was illegitimate.

Helen is half faerie, and not quite wholly rooted in her life raised amongst humans. She feels she was never quite accepted by the townspeople, since they were aware that magic and the woods had something to do with her mysterious arrival.

Helen is in many ways the polar opposite of Hermia. She is a rough and tumble, "let's go do it!" type, what we might call a tomboy.

She is drawn to Peter, because she feels how alike they are. Where Hermia loves Lyle after years of acquaintance, note that Helen is in love with a man who just showed up recently. She is spontaneous, where Hermia is steadfast. Helen is obsessed, almost to the point she can be called a stalker. She knows she is making a fool of herself by throwing herself at Peter, but doesn't care about how it looks to others, or even how it looks to Peter. Love is blind and illogical; where Hermia loves the man she has known forever, Helen's love is in stark contrast, but no less legitimate to her (or Peter).

LYLE - The boy next door, literally. He and Hermia grew up playmates, although he was not royal - merely the son of the local rug weaver (Bottom).

Lyle has grown up playing with the Duke's daughter, but also grounded well with the town's trades people as one of them. Rug weaving is the presumed future life for Lyle, although Bottom urges him to think bigger. Lyle is torn between his love for the woman above him and his feelings of inadequacy as a lowly townsman.

PETER - Helen's true match: he moves before he thinks and is quick to get dirty.

Peter is half faerie. While he has no problem in the human world and is eloquent (perhaps even because of his faerie roots), Peter loves the outdoors and wants more than anything to go out and enjoy nature.

He is also a good son and wants to follow his mother's directions, which is why he goes along with her schemes at first. He woos Hermia because that seems like what he must do, but hates himself for rejecting Helen.

PHILO – The Duke's right hand man, his clerk, serving as master of ceremonies for the wedding celebrations. Philo starts simply as an administrative member of the Duke's court, and becomes one of the play's clowns.

His "nuttiness" is shown by the exuberance in which he carries out his master's orders. He goes all in when sent to capture Lyle, by getting a net and chasing him through the woods. Also, at the end, he tackles Bottom for what he sees as the need to protect his Duke. This exuberance is what Puck recognizes, and why Puck changes him into a nut.

Underlying Philo's need to serve is his fear of getting it wrong, which Puck plays on by turning others into squirrels to chase the Nut. Philo wants to look good, just as much as does Bottom.

BOTTOM – Chief of the clowns. Such a pompous ass that Puck turns him into an ass, literally. Bottom is courageous, outgoing, and supremely confident in his acting abilities even though his acting is horrible. That he has won awards for acting merely establishes that he is the best actor among others who are even worse. But he believes he is the best, a true "triple threat" able to act, dance and sing better than anyone.

Being recognized and praised is the ultimate driving force for Bottom. "Exposure" (being seen on stage) is infinitely better to him than monetary payment.

Bottom's heart and true self is revealed through his connection to his son, Lyle. He urges Lyle to have the courage to rise above his station, while proud to leave his rug-making business to him as a viable living. But then he freaks out when he sees Lyle sitting "with the quality" because he's afraid of repercussions.

He cares for his son, but note that after he learns of Lyle's wedding he focuses immediately on how that improves his own station!

QUINCE – Clown director, and chief foil to Bottom. Quince is grounded (for example, wanting payment for his acting). He is practical, wanting to get the show done, and willing to put up with the antics of his star actor (Bottom) but tries to reel him in and get him back on point. He lives in this world and his horrified at evidence of the supernatural.

SNUG – the pitiable man with a stuttering problem, such an easy target. But he has heart! When things get ugly in their performance, Snug bravely stands in front of the Duke to help his friends (the other Players).

FLUTE

– Men had to play women, in Shakespeare's time. Now, any of these clown roles could be cast by women, but it would be good to keep the roles masculine to fit with that history. (I'd find it even funnier if a woman played a man, playing a woman – bit of a *Victor Victoria* vibe.) Flute's breaking voice can be used to heighten the comedy of each line.

Don't miss that this play has a love scene: Pyramus and Thisbe kissing through the chink in the wall. This is a moment that can be milked royally. Perhaps they struggle to reach each other, or perhaps the opposite is true: they might be able to do more than kiss! Depending upon what the "chink" is, this sight gag is wonderful.

So, too, is Thisbe's attack by the lion a chance for great slapstick comedy.

STOUT & STARVELING

– The other clowns playing actors (actors playing clowns!). These two are not well defined, so it's up to you to bring something special to the stage.

As themselves, these two are straightforward tradesmen: Stout a tailor, and Starveling a tinker (one who crafts and mends metal objects). They shine as players, with Stout become "Wall" and Starveling playing "Moonshine."

Search on YouTube and Google and you will find various examples of how Wall has been played, specifically the chink. Two fingers may be held out, or arms; at least once, the chink has been the gap between Wall's legs.

Moonshine's lantern may be big or small, and he carries a bush for unknown reason. In the original, he also had a dog – feel free to take a dog with you, if available. If so, I suggest adding the underlined new lines:

PETER
He dare not climb in, for the candle would snuff.

HELEN
And the dog? Is there a dog in the moon?

STOUT
The dog is my sister's. I'm just watching him.

LYLE
Proceed, Moon.

And then, let the dog go crazy, if it's so inclined, when Bottom grabs Lyle. (How many remember, from the movie *Shakespeare in Love*, the line, "That's what they want. Love, and a bit with a dog"?)

EXTRAS – Faeries, Lords, and Attendants,

those who in the background and scattered to the sides are so valuable to fleshing out the stage world. This play can be performed without any such, but it shows better with extras adding life to each scene.

Queen Titania's faeries may be more than those named. She may have more attendants, for what queen goes about without her women in waiting? Likewise, King Oberon may seem more kingly, were he to have one or more guards with him.

For larger productions with expansive stages and a plethora of available actors, there is the idea that Queen Titania has not only withheld sex from her husband but also commanded all faeries to withhold affection from the King's men. That is already presented here through Blossom's reaction to Puck, and in the way Cobweb must sneak off to be with Puck. But this theme can be easily expanded with male faeries and female faeries held apart, and only coming together when Titania removes her edict. Faerie couples dancing together would be a good addition to the end.

Mention is made of the lords and "finest nobles" coming to celebrate the Duke's wedding. Depending upon the size of stage and the number of actors available, this is a situation where the-more-the-merrier truly applies.

Mention is also made of other entertainment acts performed for the Duke in Act 5. Perhaps some such would be visible on the sides. It would be fun to add jugglers, dancers, animal handlers, painted ladies, pink elephants ....

Set Design Notes

Shakespeare's plays are written, mostly, for actors performing in the round with little to no actual set. *MSND* is no exception. It is an easy play to put on with a minimal set. That said, however, a nicer set will provide evidence of the faeries magic, as they spread their faerie dust to awaken the natural beauty. Hopefully, the set will help lend a feeling of wonder and magic.

MSND takes place mostly in the forest, or outdoors at least in nature. Could be a field, a swamp, even a desert. There are many references to being "in the Woods", which can be interpreted as about anything natural. Acts 2, 3, and 4 are in the Woods. There needs be 2 or 3 different areas, so that actors can be moving through the woods, at times hiding from each other.

Acts 1 and 5 are in Athens, by which I mean these acts are set where people reside – the opposite of nature. One set could do for both acts entirely, even just a large wall.

Production Notes

To be more distinctive, however, consider the need for the following areas:

Act 1 Sc. 2 — Puck and the faeries would meet in a field or garden in Athens, away from townspeople. If Puck has come forward for his prologue, the faeries may just join him there. A backdrop of mist may be enough to place Puck and the faeries away from civilization.

Act 1 Sc. 3 — Bottom's rug store, where he makes and sells rugs. He is a weaver. There can be a rug hanging, or many rugs, or even go so far as to include a proper loom.

Act 1 Sc. 4 — The Duke's palace. This should be a wide area, for the Duke's court (nobles, visitors, clerks, etc.)

Act 5 — Also the Duke's palace, but could instead be a field, as a wedding reception is often outdoors.

Production License

Shakespeare's play is in the public domain, but this version of it has been created by Brent Nautic Von Horn, who holds all copyright and all rights to performance. (Though, of course, no rights are claimed to Shakespeare's characters and words.)

All rights to perform *Doable Midsummer Night's Dream* on stage for a live audience will be granted to you, almost free of charge, provided:

>	1. you request a license to use this work from the author at the following email address:
>
>		nauticproductions@yahoo.com
>
>	2. you (or your production) purchase at

least ten (10) or more copies of the paperback version of this book *Doable Midsummer Night's Dream* from the author (you'll need at least 10 copies of the script for your actors)

3. you send at least 3 pictures of your production to the author's email address above; <u>and</u>

4. that you give credit to the author (Brent Nautic Von Horn) in some nice manner (preferably in your play's program, though on your poster or even in sky writing would be really nice, too).

ALL OTHER RIGHTS are expressly retained by the author, including (without limitation) all rights to film, record, broadcast, stream, or present this work in any manner other than a live performance as above.

www.ingramcontent.com/pod-product-compliance
Lightning Source LLC
Chambersburg PA
CBHW061324040426
42444CB00011B/2771